WELCOME TO
MY **GREAT** LIFE

ARE YOU READY FOR THE **GREAT** LIFE?

LARGE FORMAT HOME EDITION
XL

"Today you are You,
that is Truer than True.
There is no one Alive
who is
Youer than You."

- Dr. Seuss

80 CENTS FROM EVERY COPY SOLD* GOES TOWARDS HELPING GREATAPE'S EVERYWHERE Thank-you

Conceptualized, Designed and Written by Mark Enright
Cover Mandala & Colourable Mandalas Hand-drawn by Jasmim Paixao

LEARN MORE ABOUT **GREAT**APE PROGRAMS, READ THE BLOG AND FIND EXTRA CONTENT AT WWW.GREATAPE.CA

*IN CANADIAN DOLLARS (CAD) PER FULL COVER PRICED COPY

WELCOME TO MY **GREAT** LIFE

THIS WORKBOOK BELONGS TO:

PRIVACY & CONFIDENTIALITY STATEMENT

This is the personal information and property of the owner stated above.

Only the owner of this workbook has permission to read or browse the contents within.

This is a personal journey and it is considered STRICTLY PRIVATE AND CONFIDENTIAL, unless stated otherwise by the owner.

Please treat the privacy of the owner how you would like to be treated; with respect and courtesy.

Your thoughtfulness is much appreciated.

MY ACKNOWLEDGMENTS

This Workbook is the combination of human collective knowledge. I did not create all of this knowledge, I learnt it, I put it into practice in my own life, I shared it with others and I'm now passing it on to you. I have researched, combined and presented this knowledge in a way that I hope you find helpful; but the content within is not all from my own head.

While I created the structure, design and thread to bring this together; it was built on the work of scholars, writers, philosophers, academics, researchers, spiritual leaders, world leaders, explorers, adventurers, civil rights leaders, inspirational figures and scientists from around Planet Earth. The content within is based on their wisdom and their words and actions, as they have worked to improve the human condition in their own way.

I have read, listened and studied both the science/academic and the religious/spiritual. From growing up in a practicing Christian household, my global explorations have led me to learn in many amazing places. From the banks of the Holy Ganges River in India, listening to Hindu Shamans; to Bodh Gaya, where Buddha gained Enlightenment under the Bodhi Tree. I would learn from Rabbis, Priests and Imams in the many holy places of Jerusalem and the Middle East. I have listened to Indigenous stories, from both Hemispheres, as I seek to understand their deep connection to place and ancestors. To the temples of Salt Lake City, Utah and the Incan Civilizations of Peru, I have always been a seeker with eyes and ears wide open.

Academically, I have a business management and leadership background. As an experienced teacher, instructor and coach, I have read and researched widely, putting theories into action; personally and with students. I'm a field researcher, I learn from books, but I gain wisdom from experience. I have studied how adults learn and the importance of 'Why?'

All specific theories, quotes and models are referenced with authors and academics included on the same page. Due to the countless sources, simply search their names / models and you will find out more information. If I were to do a true reference page, it would be longer than this book and impossible to finish.

I encourage critical thinking and creative thinking. I don't expect, nor want you to blindly follow, you're free and welcome to disagree and come to your own thoughtful conclusions. Different opinions are good. Debate is good. That's how I believe we all make things better. But this is only possible if you have accurate information and respectful discourse.

My aim is not to impart on to you anything but the knowledge and experiences I have learned on my life's journey thus far. I've turned this into my own wisdom and now I'm openly sharing, so these pages may be of help to you. I'm being vulnerable in doing this, but it's worth the risk. As I know first-hand, the importance of creating meaningful values and living a life with purpose and conviction; not someone else's, your own. The only thing I hope from this book is that it helps you on your journey, in finding your own purpose and to live your own Great Life!

My heartfelt thanks to all those who inspired and helped me on my journey; my teachers, professors, mentors, colleagues, neighbours, guides, family, friends, and partner. Without all of you, this would not even be a dream and I'm forever grateful.

To all the Creative, Curious and Compassionate humans trying to genuinely improve their own lives and that of others; this is dedicated to you and your Quest.

Journey on!
Mark

MY ACKNOWLEDGMENTS

ACKNOWLEDING & RESPECTING PLACE & THE PEOPLE WHO HAVE LIVED ON THE LAND BEFORE YOU. APPRECIATING YOUR PLACE & ALL THOSE WHO WILL COME AFTER. IT'S "RESPECT OF PLACE".
WE ARE ALL STEWARDS FOR FUTURE GENERATIONS.

I would like to acknowledge that this workbook was created on the traditional and unceded territories of the Coast Salish people - Squamish Sḵwx̱wú7mesh and Li'lwat Lil̓wat7úl First Nations.

It is with great respect that I live on their ancestral lands, which they have stewarded for thousands of years. The beauty and wild of British Columbia, Canada have been a true inspiration in the creation of the contents within.

APPRECIATING & RESPECTING MY PLACES

"INUKSUK"

INUKSUK ARE USED BY THE INUIT ACTIC PEOPLES FOR NAVIGATION, AS A POINT OF REFERENCE, TO MARK FISHING PLACES, CAMPS, HUNTING GROUNDS, SACRED PLACES & STORAGE LOCATIONS.

WELCOME TO MY **GREAT** LIFE

CONTENTS - WHAT LIES WITHIN...

HOME EDITION
MAGAZINE SIZE
BIGGER PRINT
MORE SPACE TO WRITE
LARGE MANDALAS TO COLOUR OR SHADE
MORE SPACE TO GROW!

MY **GREAT** LIFE

MY ALIGNMENT & EQUILIBRIUM

MY LIFE VALUES

MY LIFE MISSION

MY LIFE 8

SPIRITUAL / ALTRUISTIC

MENTAL

SOCIAL

INTIMATE

TECHNOLOGICAL

WORK / CREATIVE

PHYSICAL

ENVIRONMENTAL

MY 16 HOURS

WORLD TIME ZONES

"Know the world in yourself. never look for yourself in the world,
for this world is to project your illusion."
- Ancient Egyptian Proverb

WELCOME TO MY **GREAT** LIFE

HELLO THERE, YES YOU! I WOULD LIKE TO START BY INTRODUCING MYSELF.

Welcome to the start of a beautiful relationship. If this book belongs to you, welcome, get comfortable, we could be together for a while.

Let me introduce myself, as I'm not your typical book you see, I'm a workbook that you complete, so that makes me a little different. Let's get acquainted!

The first thing is, I can only belong to one person. Once your name graces my pages, I am yours and yours alone. Yes, it's just you and me. Because actually, I'm much more than just a workbook, I'm your companion on a journey. Well, that's if you choose to continue of course. As choice is a big part of this journey. You'll be making a lot of choices, as this is not someone else's adventure; this is Your Story.

Of course, we can share our adventure with others too, if you like? We can also work with professionals or in a trusted group too.

'My Great Life' is all about you. Yes you, the one who is reading this. We're here together on a quest towards living intentionally, creating Your Great Life. Not by magic tricks and get-rich-quick schemes, but by simple and sound guidance from your human collective knowledge & experience. 'You' will become 'Me', so this story becomes; 'My Great Life'. That's what we are doing here, you and me, working to create your own Great Life, one step at a time.

> **THE AIM OF THIS BOOK:**
> TO BE YOUR COMPANION ON YOUR JOURNEY TOWARDS YOUR MOST FULFILLING & BALANCED LIFE

I'm warning you though, it's not an easy journey, it's filled with obstacles and adventure. I'm not sure where this journey will take us, the exact destination is unknown. But rest assured, I'll be at your side. I'll be here for you to return to and think with; to laugh with, cry with and share with. I'm a great listener, but my feedback can be slow, although it may take some time, it will come. Good things take time and effort; well, that's what my creator told me to tell you.

Most of the time, what I have to say, in the words and quotes within, is to help you answer your own questions. It won't always be clear, nor easy at first, but keep at it and over time, with consideration, your answers will come. I mean, you're the best person to answer your own questions, as you're really the only one who knows the answers.

I'm here for you. To help explore your answers. If it helps, you can give me a name. I don't much like the name 'Workbook', if that's too weird this early in our relationship? I understand, but feel free to give me a name at a later date.

> **TIME TO COMPLETE:**
> FROM 2 WEEKS TO 1 LIFETIME

So more about me; inside you'll find various tools, techniques and strategies to stimulate your thoughts, feelings, creativity, communication, goals, habits and routines. It's about helping you take practical steps to create new opportunities for growth and trigger positive action. Does that sound like something you'd like to work on? If it does, I can tell you, we're in for quite the ride! I don't want to scare you, but really; you can change your whole world, if that's what you want?

WELCOME TO MY **GREAT** LIFE

I also have a sense of humour, so feel free to share. I'm gender-neutral, in-fact I'm everything neutral. I'm more neutral than Switzerland, but with less yodeling. I never said I was funny! It's just... I also like to see you laugh. And although we'll be tackling some serious issues, I want you to always remember, as my friend Mickey Mouse once said; 'To laugh at yourself is to love yourself' (Walt Disney). I love that advice, so instead of taking everything too seriously, you also need to see the light, the joy, the funny side at times. Do we have a deal?

Like I said, I'm neutral, some quotes inside are using masculine nouns and pronouns (Man, He, His etc.) but that's not my fault, as I'm just repeating exactly how it was said by the person who said it. But I want to assure you, I (this book) was created and intended for Everyone. I'm inclusive; whatever your political persuasion, religious ideology or lifestyle choice; the information inside is for ALL humans, however you identify, whomever you love, come as you are, you are always welcome here.
With me, you can be your genuine-self! In-fact, that's what I'm here for; for you to be... you.

I'm here to be written on, I'm not some book that sits idle on a shelf, I'm here to be part of the action and used on your quest for Greatness. Dog ears look good on me! Writing on me will help you because I don't forget, (unless you erase it) so I can be a storage and reminder for you, I also don't need a battery!

We're doing this together, you and me, and I'll be here to support you in keeping your worlds aligned, while reminding you of the most important parts of your life. And if anything changes, well, I'll change with you.

As a workbook, I have also seen the benefits when you humans leave your work and come back to review it with a 'fresh pair of eyes'. By working as a team, I give you a chance to organize your thoughts on very important areas of your life, but also come back to them for more thoughtful examination and to build upon.

INSPIRATION & IDEAS

As an experienced workbook, I've found that sometimes things are found out in "Eureka" moments of inspiration, but more often, they're built up slowly over time and with further consideration, building on past ideas.
I can help you do this building.

"EUREKA" MOMENTS

SLOWLY BUILDS OVER TIME & CONSIDERATION

There is one other thing I need to warn you about on our journey together. It's pretty big! Are you ready for it? That is; you may never reach your destination!
Wow, that's not an easy statement I know, but just hear me out. I also know the next question you'll ask, 'what's the point of a journey without a destination?'
That one's simple. Everything!

Your destination will always be ahead of you, with each new goal you achieve, or milestone met, a new one takes its place. The only destination is the journey itself. That means enjoying the path and the many exciting and beautiful viewpoints on the way. My sincere hope is that by working together, you'll stop, enjoy and appreciate those many beautiful, irreplaceable moments on your unique way. Oh! That gives me goosebumps, well figuratively speaking, I am a book after all!

"Men go abroad to wonder at the
height of the mountains,
at the huge waves of the sea,
at the long courses of the rivers,
at the circular motions of the stars,
and they pass by themselves without
wondering."

-St. Augustine of Hippo

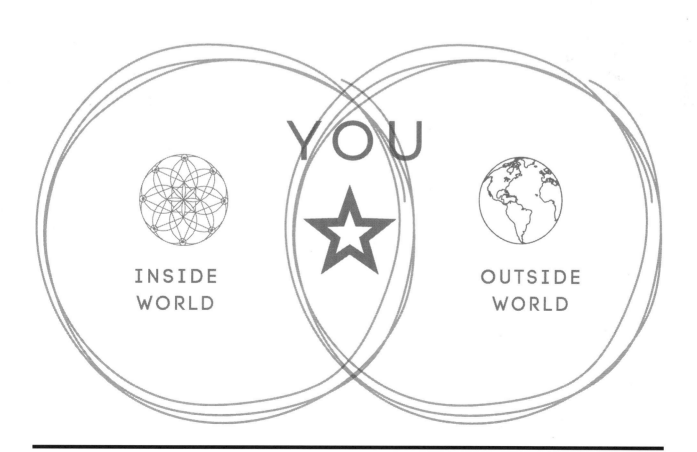

INSIDE WORLD

YOU

OUTSIDE WORLD

WELCOME TO MY **GREAT** LIFE

Here's the deal, this is why our relationship is different, it's unique. This is no fantasy novel or fairytale, it's the Greatest Story ever told, Your Story! That's my personal opinion anyway. By examining your own story, through the questions I ask, statements I pose and knowledge I share, you're getting a better grasp and understanding of yourself. I just ask; it's you who provides the answers!

I've been to many places, researched many things and I've found humans to be quite extraordinary. I think that's the only real word that I can think of to describe you, the Human Being, the Great Ape, yes, you!

Number-one, you created me! Wow, that's kind-of mind-blowing!? Anyway, to the point, humans are extremely adaptable, resilient, brave, heroic and strong. The human race has adapted to live almost everywhere, has innovated to solve problems and created the most incredible buildings, structures and artworks. I'm not saying this hasn't been without its problems, but still, the feats that I've seen in humanity have been quite, what's the word? Extraordinary!

In fact, I've found you humans to be so inspiring, from all countries, cultures, ethnic backgrounds and beliefs, that I just had to share my findings with you. I found these in books and in research papers, on blogs, on websites and through my own bookish experience. But I didn't want to be just for scientists or professors to understand, I wanted to be for anyone to use and, hopefully, get benefit from.

That's why I am very visual, I'm designed to be simple, yet I'm quite complex! I know! It can get messy at times. By bringing together important psychological, sociological, economic and physical models and guidelines, I have simplified them, so you, the human, can bring these findings into your real, Great Life.

There is one big limitation though... I'm just a book; a cool book, and quite pretty, but still, just a book. I wish I could do more, but that's outside my power. While I'm always here to help, I can't do it for you. For this relationship to truly flourish, you're the only one who can make it a reality.

My personal 'book-goal' is for you to turn these pages into your real life. I can come with you, I can support you, I am quite small and you can take me by the hand anytime. If you need some quiet time, time to reflect, well that's what I'm here for, decisions to be made, issues to overcome; I might be able to help, but it's you who needs to act on it. And remember, our aim is a Great Life, not a perfect one.

I understand that all humans have struggles and faults. As a book, you might find a spelling mistake or a grammatical error, or you may not be fond of my beautiful artworks, but that's okay, perfection is not a reality anyway! And I know for sure you can't please everyone! I believe it was one of your great scientists who said that "Nothing is perfect, perfection simply doesn't exist, without imperfection, neither you nor I would exist". Stephen Hawking was his name, just one of the many inspirational humans I've found. But do you see how crazy that is?! Thank goodness for your human imperfections, as without them, I wouldn't be here and nor would you!

Are you scared yet? I hope not! Butterflies maybe? We'll get to that later. So let's get to it, I have a special structure that you should be aware of, so read on explorer...

YOUR GREAT LIFE INTO MY **GREAT** LIFE

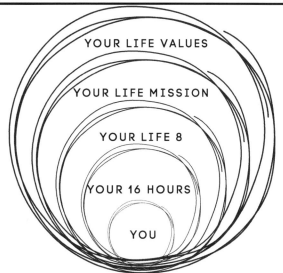

Although you can start anywhere in the book, there is a framework and structure for you to understand. I want to ensure you get the most from your journey.

I do repeat myself at times and through images, but that's because we all learn differently, and my repetitive nagging helps! Well that's what I like to believe! And although it may not help you, it can be helpful to others. You may also notice I'm rather fond of circles, mandalas and spirals, these all have meaning and you'll discover these on the way.

Look at the 'Circle', I've chosen it because it's a universal symbol, all cultures attach meaning to it. It can represent; wholeness, the lifecycle, the circle of life, the Self, the infinite, eternity, timelessness, the sun, stars and planets, all cyclic movement, God.... Yeah, so the circle is a big deal across humanity, that's why you will see a lot of it.

The overarching guidance for your life are Your Values. I will talk about them more in that section, but throughout this journey you will be creating and updating yours. You can do this at the start, or this whole journey can be about creating your values. These, like the circles in the sky, can offer you guidance throughout your life course.

Within your values system you also need a direction, stars are great in the sky, but they won't help you navigate anywhere if you don't move. Your Life Mission is about that movement. In this section you will create your own thoughtful mission, philosophy or constitution, as the compass on your journey.

Life8 is your Life, broken-down into 8 Worlds. It provides a base knowledge of the 8 key areas of importance in your life today. Inspired by the wisdom and knowledge of our global collective culture; East and West; Science, Spirituality and Philosophy. Our aim here is a greater self-awareness and understanding, while also ensuring alignment.

The final chapter, My 16 Hours is about bringing your 8 Worlds into your real life.
How do we do that? With your time. With your 16 hours you'll create World Time Zones, to stay in balance and bring all your Worlds to Life!

WELCOME TO MY **GREAT** LIFE

As you notice by the diagram illustrating the structure of this book, you'll see that the circles are also in alignment. This is part of our continuing journey and another part of the puzzle of life, aligning your worlds with your mission and values. This ensures your energies are going in the same direction, but also in the right direction!

Some of my pages and areas will be more useful to you than others, depending on your needs. Sometimes the value of it will not be known to you until after you complete it. A deeper insight, a better grasp on the problem, a solution to take action. You may be surprised where this journey will take you.

'ALIGNMENT'
A POSITION OF AGREEMENT OR ALLIANCE. THE CORRECT RELATIVE POSITION

I also want to assure you, on your journey, there's no need to completely re-invent your life. It's amazing the difference a few small tweaks and changes can make. These little improvements and small goals achieved will add up and can change your life dramatically over the long-term. Of course, that's not to say you can't re-invent your life too, if that's what you need, let's do it! We can be many things together.

All I know for sure, is that by investing in your strong, growing, resilient-self now, you're investing in your future health and wealth. I've seen it before. Don't forget, many people have walked before you and we can all learn a lot from their footsteps.

By working together we are seeking to understand yourself on a deeper level. Your overarching aim is living in harmony with your values and taking thoughtful action.
You can create a life that reflects who you really are.

LARGE MANDALAS TO COLOUR OR SHADE

Your Great Life can only be created by you, but it is not created in isolation. Not only do you have me to help you on your way, but as social creatures, you humans rely and need the love and care of each other. You can choose to take this journey alone, in positive solitude or bring some friends along for the ride.

When you see this Scale below, it represents a Continuum. with extremes at both ends, most things actually lie somewhere in between. But that's for you to decide. Mark where you think you belong - this may change over time.

HERE ——————————————————— THERE

YOU WILL ALSO SEE LOTS OF QUOTES FROM INSPIRATIONAL HUMANS TO INSPIRE YOUR OWN JOURNEY

WHEN YOU SEE THIS STAR, YOU'RE IN THE "SWEET SPOT".

WHEN YOU SEE THIS ∞ EXAMPLE IT'S AN EXAMPLE TO HELP YOU ON YOUR WAY

"I am my own Muse, I am the subject I know best.
The subject I want to know better." - Frida Kahlo (Painter)

WELCOME TO MY **GREAT** LIFE

As the famous saying by another great human thinker, Socrates, said:
"The unexamined life is not worth living." I must admit, it holds some truth. But this wisdom too, needs to be seen in context and balance.

Your personal self-development requires you to develop a strong self-awareness. For you to grow, you must have an understanding and knowledge of yourself, a baseline to grow from. The important step of developing your self awareness will help you reach your potential and live the life you want to live; BUT, yes, there is always a but; you must be careful NOT to take this to extremes.

The danger often lies in the extremes, whether that be in the absence of something or in the over-consumption of something else. From the virtuous middle path in Buddhism to the scientific proven theories on the importance of moderation, be that the amount of water you drink, kale you consume, or the video games you play. On this journey, you are seeking a balanced, middle path.

I can tell you from research conducted across thousands of years. Your aim is somewhere in the Middle. It sounds simple, it is simple, and this is all part of our journey, to find the areas which are in the extremes and look for ways you can find a better middle ground.

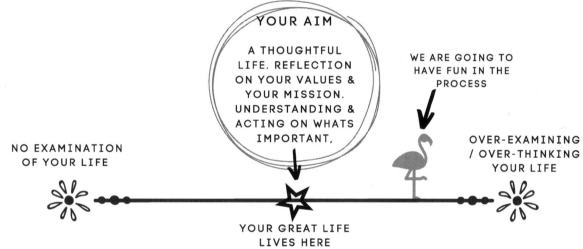

YOUR AIM

A THOUGHTFUL LIFE. REFLECTION ON YOUR VALUES & YOUR MISSION. UNDERSTANDING & ACTING ON WHATS IMPORTANT,

WE ARE GOING TO HAVE FUN IN THE PROCESS

NO EXAMINATION OF YOUR LIFE

OVER-EXAMINING / OVER-THINKING YOUR LIFE

YOUR GREAT LIFE LIVES HERE

My pages have taught me, the best way to learn something is to teach it. I know how much I learn from guiding you, but you can also learn a lot from yourself. You're going to be your own teacher through these pages. By reflecting on these questions or statements, you're connecting dots, figuring it out and coming to your own well thought-out conclusions. Don't worry, I have faith in you!

A life coach helps their client by helping them, help themselves. Learn from yourself. Learn from the things in your past that have and haven't worked. Learn from your experiences and develop your own wisdom from the human collective.

And don't forget the good advice my tree ancestors passed on to me, I'm from nature too don't forget. All this knowledge remains empty unless it's acted upon.
I'm only useful if what you learn from me, you put in practice, in that real human life of yours. My tree friends are also requesting a visit sometime...

MY RESISTANCE

On this Great Life Expedition we're on, we're exploring all your worlds and creating better alignment. It's important that you don't ignore any of your worlds, as understanding them all is part of the Holistic or Full Life growth process.

As you'll have your strengths, you'll also have your weaknesses. Facing things you may not want to face will cause you discomfort at times and that won't always be fun. You're likely to come across 'resistance' during your journey. It's not going to be a carefree and 'easy' ride all the time. The resistance that you encounter could be coming from the area you're working on as it is a 'Pain Point', an area which you have issues to confront. It's natural you will push back.

Where you're holding back, you may feel discomfort. That's not a bad thing. Here you'll have to manage your resistance. Sometimes you'll have to put me (this book) down, go away and have a long walk or speak to a close friend and then come back and try again. Your holding back shouldn't be interpreted as something wrong, rather it may mean you have found areas where you may need to focus and work on. The areas in which this exploration will help you the most, are the areas you probably like the least.

"RESIST"
COMES FROM LATIN - "RE SISTERE" WHICH MEANS "HOLD BACK".

TIME AND TIME AGAIN YOU ARE LIKELY TO COME ACROSS YOUR OWN RESISTANCE

Your "holding back" can also be as a result of a word that will come up again and again on this journey, 'Vulnerability'. Writing down some of your closest thoughts, desires, dreams and values will be very difficult for some, or at some times. Writing down what is somewhere swirling inside you and putting that onto paper is not easy and it may make you feel you are opening yourself up for attack.

Being vulnerable is not a weakness, in-fact, it takes courage and bravery to be emotionally vulnerable, as it means you are trying to become your authentic self. Your aim is to become resilient, strong and authentic. To be truly vulnerable you also have to be honest with yourself. That honesty does not always come easy, or quickly.

"VULNERABLE"
THE FEELING OF BEING EXPOSED & OPEN TO ATTACK FOR BEING YOUR TRUE SELF.

There is great value in writing these things down but that's not a necessity. You can choose to read and think of your answers, or write them down on a separate piece of paper and throw it away. If you feel too vulnerable to write your answers down, use your voice recorder to speak your answers. You may wish to draw pictures, symbols or doodle in the spaces. What is important, is that you feel safe and secure while pushing out of your personally defined 'comfort zone'. It'll take effort and it won't always be easy but I know you can do it! Go on, you are braver than you think!

"RESILIENT"
RECOVER, WITHSTAND & BOUNCE-BACK FROM SET- BACKS & NEGATIVE EVENTS

"The path of least resistance leads to crooked rivers and crooked men." - Henry David Thoreau (Writer)

"Reflect upon your present blessings, of which every (wo)man has plenty; not on your past misfortunes, of which all (wo)men have some."

- Charles Dickens

THIS QUOTE HAS BEEN UPDATED TO BE MORE INCLUSIVE & REFLECTIVE OF THE FULL POPULATION.
IT'S THE ONLY PLACE THE ORIGINAL FORMAT HAS BEEN ADDED TO.
MANY OF THE QUOTES WITHIN ARE IN THE ORIGINAL MASCULINE FORMAT. BUT HERE ON MY PAGES,
ALWAYS REMEMBER - "MAN" MEANS "HUMAN" & 'HIS'-STORY IS ALSO 'HER'-STORY.

GRATITUDE IS ONE OF THE HEALTHIEST OF ALL HUMAN EMOTIONS.
THIS PAGE IS AT THE BEGINNING TO HIGHLIGHT ITS IMPORTANCE IN ALL
YOUR WORLDS. WHAT ARE YOU GRATEFUL FOR? WHO DO YOU APPRECIATE?

MY LIFE VALUES

"Keep your thoughts positive because
your thoughts become
YOUR WORDS.

Keep your words positive
because your words become
YOUR BEHAVIOUR.

Keep your behaviour positive because
your behaviour becomes
YOUR HABITS.

Keep your habits positive
because your habits become
YOUR VALUES.

Keep your values positive
because your values become
YOUR DESTINY."

- Mahatma Gandhi

MY LIFE 8 VALUES

Your Values are important. They are the key qualities that make you; You. They are your building blocks, your life is built on the foundation of your values. How strong is your foundation?

Your values will guide your decisions, influence your motivations and determine whether you'll take action. They're personal, they're yours and though they may change and adapt over time, no one can take your values from you.

Although you may not label them as 'values', you live your life to a personal code of conduct, your own expectations, your own rules and perspective as to what is right and what is best for your life and those around you. Basically, your values are the unwritten rules in which you live your life.

You chose not to steal me - this book, (I hope) because honesty is probably, somehow, a value to you. You don't need to be religious, have a dogma or constitution, but it's good to have something to base your existence on. Something to guide your actions and behaviours for what you want and expect for yourself.

Your Life Values are simply the guidelines you set for yourself on a daily basis, it's your moral and ethical code to live how you choose to live. Your values are not created in isolation, they're passed on to you and learned from your culture and the people around you.

To illustrate this further, let's look at Superheroes; Batman, Wonder Woman or The Hulk. Each of these heroes have a strong values-based system, fighting against evil, helping the innocent, saving lives. If your favourite hero had no values, he/she/it would likely be causing chaos and stealing all your money; is that something you would look up to? Movies and TV shows, if anything, show this 'value-based' system is alive and well in humanity and how we expect our heroes to behave, super or otherwise.

"VALUES"

AN INDIVIDUAL'S PRINCIPLES OR STANDARDS OF BEHAVIOUR; ONE'S JUDGEMENT OF WHAT'S IMPORTANT IN LIFE.

If superheroes aren't your thing, go into the real world and still you will see the impact of values. Think about the people from the past or present who inspire you? Who do you look up to? Chances are, they have a very strong values-based life. From Nelson Mandela, Florence Nightingale, to Martin Luther King Jr. You likely respect these historical figures for their strong values; values which they risked their lives and reputations on. They lived their values and gained the world's respect as a result.

That's the importance of values and that's why you too can benefit from creating your own values to live by.

"I think the Greatest of people that have been in society, they were never versions of someone else. They were themselves."
- Neil deGrasse Tyson (Astrophysicist, Author, Educator)

MY LIFE 8 VALUES

Here, you'll create Eight (8) Basic Life Values. These values should be words of deep meaning and connection for you.

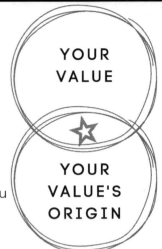

YOUR VALUE

YOUR VALUE'S ORIGIN

The aim here is to BOTH; identify 8 of your core values, AND; think about who or where each of these came from. By doing this you're creating a stronger personal connection to that value. You're much more likely to actively live by a value if you also know where it came from, or where it's inspired from. Give each of your values an 'Origin Story'.

It may be hard to pinpoint exactly where your values come from, but you probably have some ideas; from the people in your life, or experiences you have had. You've been inspired by them, they become more than words and part of you.

Your goal here is not an empty list of beautiful words on the page. You can write anything that sounds good. It must be meaningful to you. By attaching an origin to the value, you create this added personal connection. You're adding concrete to that value, as you know why you have it and where it came from. Once you know this, it will become part of you and easier to recall and act on.

Most people know they have values, they just have not identified or articulated them.
It doesn't have to be all at once. Make it a journey, meditate on words, think about them. And if you have really never thought about your values, here's a chance to shape your world in a truly meaningful way.

'My Life Values' are at the very start of my pages, not because you need to do this first; they're at the start of the book because they're so important!

As you work through my pages, using the 'Brainstorm' page, as well as the word list to help with inspiration; create as many values as suits your life - 8 is a good amount, but like everything here, that's completely up to you!

They can be values that you feel you possess, or are working and aspiring towards.
The aim isn't perfection, or rigorous rules to live by (they can be of course), but simply identifying what's really meaningful to you - will help guide you in living your Great Life.

Your Values are the stars that provide guidance to your own life, not how others should live theirs. Your Values aren't there to be pushed onto others. You own, are as unique and personal as everyone else's .

Here you need to be genuine with yourself. Take control of this most important part of your life. Spend some time and create meaningful Life Values for "My Great Life".

"Values are like fingerprints. Nobody's are the same, but you leave 'em all over everything you do."
- Elvis Presley ("King" of Rock 'n Roll)

MY LIFE 8 VALUES

MY LIFE VALUES*

MY VALUE 'ORIGIN STORY'

*MY VALUES =
MY JUDGEMENT
OF WHAT I SEE
AS IMPORTANT
IN LIFE

1

2

3

4

5

6

7

8

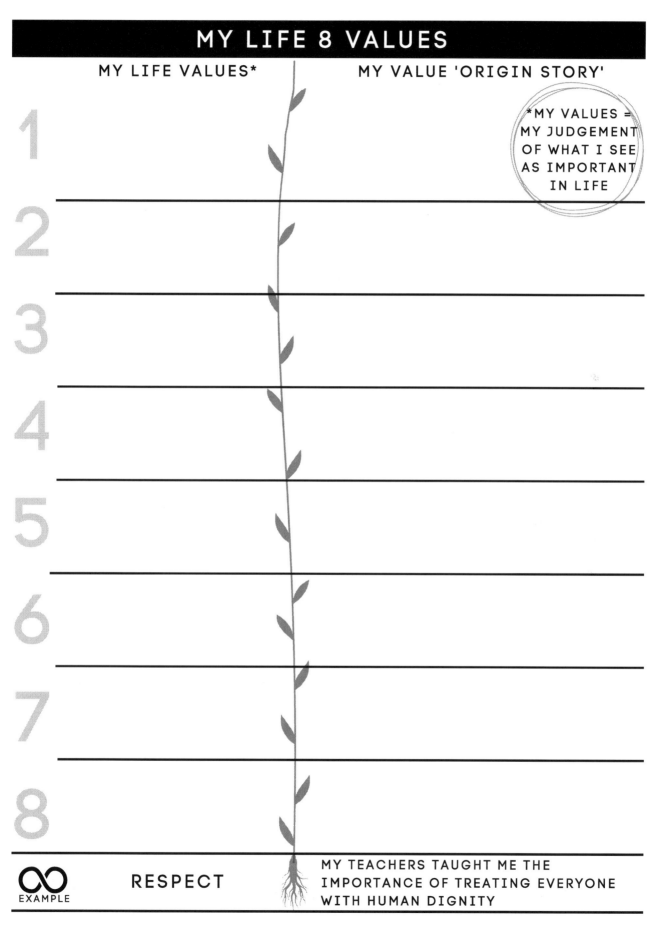

∞
EXAMPLE

RESPECT

MY TEACHERS TAUGHT ME THE
IMPORTANCE OF TREATING EVERYONE
WITH HUMAN DIGNITY

MY LIFE 8 VALUES - BRAINSTORM

ABUNDANCE	FUN	SPIRITUALITY
ACCEPTANCE	FAITH	STABILITY
ACCOUNTABILITY	FAMILY	STRENGTH
ACHIEVEMENT	FREINDSHIPS	SUPPORT
ADVANCEMENT	FIDELITY	PEACE
ADVENTURE	GENEROSITY	PERFECTION
ADVOCACY	GRACE	PLAYFULNESS
AMBITION	GRATITUDE	POPULARITY
APPRECIATION	GROWTH	POWER
ATTRACTIVENESS	FLEXIBILITY	POISE
AUTONOMY	HAPPINESS	PREPAREDNESS
AWE	HEALTH	PROACTIVITY
BALANCE	HONESTY	PROFESSIONALISM
BEING THE BEST	HUMILITY	PUNCTUALITY
BENEVOLENCE	HOSPITALITY	PERSERVERANCE
BOLDNESS	HUMOUR	REASON
BRILLIANCE	INCLUSIVENESS	RECOGNITION
CALMNESS	INDEPENDENCE	RELATIONSHIPS
CARING	INDIVIDUALITY	RELIABILITY
CHALLENGE	INNOVATION	RESILIENCE
CHARITY	IMAGINATION	RESOURCEFULNESS
CHEERFULNESS	INSPIRATION	RESPONSIBILITY
CLEVERNESS	INTEGRITY	RECREATION
COMMUNITY	INTELLIGENCE	RECOGNITION
COMMITMENT	INTUITION	RESPONSIVENESS
COMPASSION	JOY	SACRIFICE
COOPERATION	JUSTICE	SECURITY
COLLABORATION	KINDNESS	SELF-CONTROL
CONSISTENCY	KNOWLEDGE	SELFLESSNESS
CONTRIBUTION	LEADERSHIP	SIMPLICITY
COURTESY	LEARNING	SINCERITY
COURAGE	LOVE	STABILITY
CONTENTMENT	LOYALTY	SUCCESS
CREATIVITY	MAKING A DIFFERENCE	TEAMWORK
CREDIBILITY	MINDFULNESS	THANKFULNESS
CURIOSITY	MOTIVATION	THOUGHTFULNESS
DARING	OPTIMISM	TRADITIONALISM
DEPTH	OPEN-MINDEDNESS	TRANQULITY
DECISIVENESS	ORIGINALITY	TRUSTWORTHINESS
DEDICATION	ORGANIZATION	UNDERSTANDING
DEPENDABILITY	PASSION	UNIQUENESS
DIVERSITY	PERFORMANCE	USEFULNESS
EMPATHY	PERSONAL DEVELOPMENT	VERSATILITY
ENCOURAGEMENT	PROACTIVE	VISION
ENTHUSIASM	PLAYFULNESS	VITALITY
ETHICAL	PLEASURE	WARMTH
EXCELLENCE	PROFESSIONALISM	WEALTH
EXPERTISE	QUALITY	WONDER
EXPERIENCE	RECOGNITION	WILLINGNESS
EXPLORATION	RISK TAKING	WELL-BEING
EXPRESSIVENESS	SAFETY	WISDOM
FAIRNESS	SECURITY	ZEAL
FLEXIBILITY	SERVICE	
FREEDOM	SENSITIVITY	

WHAT IS MOST
IMPORTANT TO ME ?

VALUE = RELATIVE WORTH, UTILITY OR IMPORTANCE ONE GIVES SOMETHING -
BOTH EXTRINSIC (MONEY & THINGS) & INTRINSIC (TRUST, COURAGE, HOPE...)
WHAT DO YOU REALLY VALUE?

MY LIFE MISSION

Your Life is a Journey...

Your values are the stars that
guide the way.

Your mission is the compass for
the path beneath your feet.

Your curiosity sparks learning
that drives your forward.

Through sunshine and rain your
courage gives you strength to
grow.

Your wisdom and experience are
honed on the way.
This is your place and your home.

Your GREAT Life is yours to
explore...

MY LIFE MISSION / PHILOSOPHY

Your Mission, it sounds rather grand, poetic and rather "Impossible" to ever know, but there is no better word to use for this purpose. Actually, there could be... read on!

Having a 'Life Mission', or finding a 'Mission in Life' is not an easy thing to do. If you're a person who knows what you're put on this earth to do and seeking out that path with conviction, you're indeed one of the lucky ones. Here, this step is easier for you.

While this may be positioned at the start of the book, it's not likely the best place to start, unless of course, this is already clearly known to you. Otherwise, create this over time and throughout your journey.

CHOOSE THE WORD THAT BEST WORKS FOR YOU:

MISSION

"A STRONGLY FELT AIM, AMBITION, OR CALLING."

PHILOSOPHY

"A THEORY OR ATTITUDE HELD THAT ACTS AS A GUIDING PRINCIPLE FOR BEHAVIOUR."

CONSTITUTION

"THE COMING TOGETHER OF GUIDING PRINCIPLES TO MAKE A WHOLE"

One of your biggest questions in life is that of your own purpose. It's a fundamental question, and while you may look at animals and see their "Ignorance is Bliss"; Great Apes, of the Human variety, want to know more. You seek further meaning in existence, seeking the answers to "why?"

In seeking your life mission, you're <u>not</u> seeking to discover 'the meaning of life', 'the 'origin of the universe', or 'the purpose of humankind'. Your Life Mission is only about seeking what you would like to do with your time on earth. Instead of going in circles, it gives direction. Circles are great for symbolism, but poor for direction!

Much like a Mission Statement gives a corporation its highest level guidance and values to uphold. Your Mission / Philosophy / Constitution should align with your values and provide your life with guidance and direction. I know, a broken-record!

A Personal Philosophy is another term you could use. While a Mission can imply a destiny and is often referenced in religious terms, 'a philosophy' is unmistakably secular. Your philosophy can be a collection of your greatest wisdom in which guides your life and the life you want to live.

Or there's a 'Constitution'; your own guiding or founding document - laws or amendments that give your life structure and meaning. If a piece of paper can shape entire countries; can you imagine what this can do for your life?

Of course, like all things, these may change and these too can be updated over time. So whether it's a Mission, Philosophy or Constitution, you're creating statements of intent and an objective for your life overall. Give your life a compass, so you can move forward with purpose and in the direction of your dreams.

MY LIFE...

MISSION - PHILOSOPHY - CONSTITUTION

CHOOSE ONE & CREATE YOURS...

"The greatest adventure is what lies ahead..." - J.R.R. Tolkien

WHAT DO I WANT TO ACHIEVE IN MY LIFE?

- Happiness
- Peace
- Calm
- Love

As a Philosopher, you're; "a Lover of Wisdom".
Creating your own Philosophy, based on your Wisdom.
With a Mission at Heart, you're Impossible to stop.
Creating yours, will take you on your Journey Home.
A Constitution gives you Presidency over your Life.
Lead the life you want, Write it down & Sign the dotted line.

"Wisdom cannot be imparted.
Wisdom that a wise man attempts to
impart always sounds like
foolishnesss to someone else ...
Knowledge can be communicated,
but not wisdom. One can find it, live
it, do wonders through it, but one
cannot communicate and teach it."

— Hermann Hesse, Siddhartha

SWISS-GERMAN POET, NOVELIST & PAINTER - WINNING THE NOBEL PRIZE FOR
LITERATURE IN 1946

MY 8 WORLDS

Spiritual / Altruistic
Purpose - Meaning - Service

Mental
Mindset - Motivation

Technological
Digital Life

Social
Communications

Intimate
Trusted Connection - Emotions

Work / Creative
Skill - Expertise - Knowledge

Physical
Bodily Awareness

Environmental
Place - Security

LEONARDO DA VINCI'S VITRUVIAN MAN

MY LIFE 8

MY 8 WORLDS

Your 8 Worlds make up Your Life. As your human life is complex, by breaking it down into Worlds, you can find simple and effective ways to think about all the most important aspects of your life; holistically. The goal here is to give you a more balanced, healthier and meaningful existence. Everyone and anyone can use the tools and techniques within to help better fulfill and align their lives.

'Holistic' comes from the word 'whole'. By looking at your whole life together, through a series of closely interconnected worlds; you'll be better able to navigate and manage the key aspects of your life. You'll also create more alignment and focus on the things that really matter. The circle symbolizes wholeness, but you already knew that!

Your 8 Worlds are based on the ancient wisdom and science of both the East and the West. Your 7 Chakras, or main energy centers, run from the top of your head down your spine and they have been studied for thousands of years, and by many cultures. They're incorporated into; Chinese medicine, Ayurvedic medicine, Buddhist teachings, Meditational practice, Yoga, Hinduism and many Spiritual philosophies.

"HOLISTIC"
=
WHOLE

"CHAKRA"
=
CIRCLE
WHEEL

These energy centers govern key aspects of your health and wellbeing and correlate to key organs in your body which are major energy systems and/or are important hormone and chemical producing glands or centers.

YOUR 7 CHAKRAS

The world today is different from our ancient past. There are vast new influences that humans now need to manage, which is why the addition of an 8th Center, the Technological.

Our aim is to help you get your 8 worlds organized. With so many thoughts, reactions, fears and dreams. Getting these out of your head and onto paper will help you see your life from a whole new perspective and more importantly, help you take action to make improvements and create the life you want.

You're not just a collection of parts. But when you look at the parts of your life separately, it means that you're likely making decisions based on the parts, not the whole. You're making decisions and reacting based on just one or two aspects of your life, instead of taking into account your full life and what's best for it.

Your 8 Worlds are about creating balance and positive change. It's based on the human collective knowledge from across the scientific spectrum and the wisdom of our collective past. So let's start your journey. Let's explore Your Worlds!

"We cannot teach people anything; we can only help them discover it within themselves. " - Galileo Galilei ("Father of Modern Science")

MY 8 WORLDS

SPIRITUAL / ALTRUISTIC

- PURPOSE
- MEANING
- SERVICE TO OTHERS
- CONNECTION TO DIVINITY
- MEDITATION / PRAYER / REFLECTION

- Do you feel your life has meaning?
- Do you appreciate your life?
- Do you help others? Without expecting anything in return?

MENTAL

- MOTIVATION
- DECISION MAKING
- FOCUS
- MINDSET
- FEARS

- What motivates you?
- What guides your decisions?
- How do you react to stress / adversity?

SOCIAL

- COMMUNICATIONS
- CONNECTIONS
- BELONGING
- NETWORK
- COMMUNITY

- Are you a respectful communicator?
- Do you listen to others? (actively?)
- Do you enjoy activities with others?

INTIMATE

- TRUST
- LOVE
- EMOTIONS
- VULNERABILITIES
- COMFORT ZONE

- Do you have a close, trusted relationship?
- Can you be yourself around others?
- Do you feel lonely?

TECHNOLOGICAL

- DIGITAL LIFE
- BEST PRACTICES
- SMARTPHONE USE
- INNOVATION
- INFORMATION

- Do you control your phone?
- Are you happy with the time you spend online?
- Does your online world reflect your offline world?

WORK / CREATIVE

- FLOW
- CAREER
- SKILL DEVELOPMENT
- CREATIVITY
- PASSIONS

- Do you have a creative outlet?
- Do you see mistakes as learning opportunities?
- Are you satisfied with your work?

PHYSICAL

- MOVEMENT
- NUTRITION
- SLEEP / RECOVERY
- STRESS / WORRY
- STRENGTH / WEAKNESS

- Do you get enough sleep?
- How are your energy levels?
- Are you conscious what you put into your body?

ENVIRONMENTAL

- NATURAL WORLD
- CULTURE
- ADVENTURE
- PLACES OF MEANING
- SAFETY / SECURITY

- Are you aware of your surroundings?
- Do you feel secure in your environment?
- Do you interact with nature?

You can take the full 8 Worlds Quiz at www.greatape.ca
It's FREE and may help guide you where you need to focus.

MY LIFE-EIGHT OUTCOMES

THE KEY OUTCOMES IN EACH OF MY WORLDS

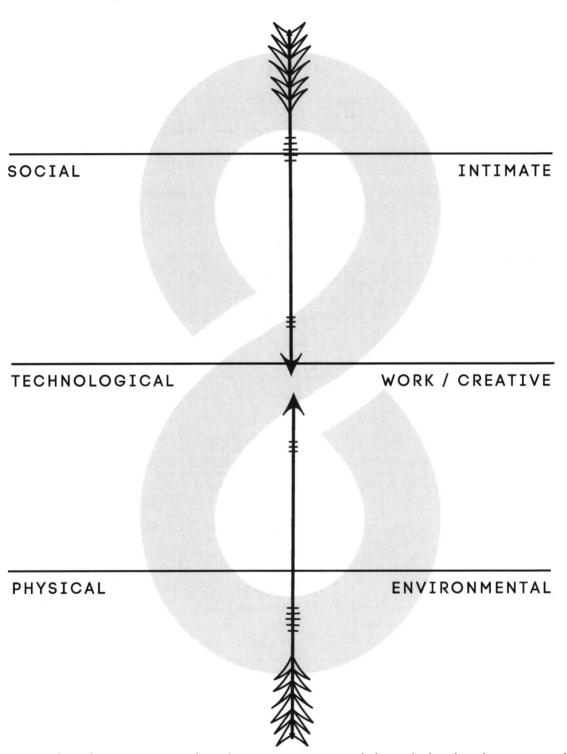

SPIRITUAL / ALTRUISTIC

MENTAL

SOCIAL

INTIMATE

TECHNOLOGICAL

WORK / CREATIVE

PHYSICAL

ENVIRONMENTAL

"It is good to have an end to journey toward; but it is the journey that matters, in the end." - Ernest Hemingway (Writer, Adventurer)

MY WORLDS ALIGNED
WHERE ARE YOU NOW? HOW I FEEL IN MY WORLDS...

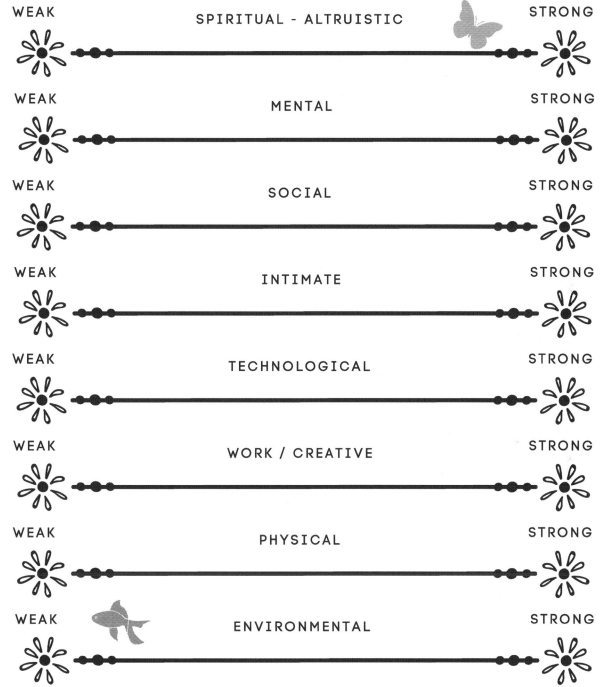

WEAK		STRONG
	SPIRITUAL - ALTRUISTIC	
	MENTAL	
	SOCIAL	
	INTIMATE	
	TECHNOLOGICAL	
	WORK / CREATIVE	
	PHYSICAL	
	ENVIRONMENTAL	

WHERE DO YOU FEEL YOU ARE FOR EACH OF YOUR WORLDS? JOIN THE DOTS AND LOOK AT THE SHAPE OF THE LINE. WHERE ARE THE AREAS FOR IMPROVEMENT? WHERE ARE YOU OUT OF ALIGNMENT? AS YOU WORK THROUGH YOUR WORLDS, WATCH THE LINE CHANGE - AS YOU TAKE BACK CONTROL & CREATE THE GREAT LIFE YOU WANT.

"Life is like a harp string, if it's strung too tight it won't play, if it's too loose it hangs, the tension that produces the beautiful sound lies in the middle." - Gautama Buddha

ENVIRONMENTAL

MY GOALS / OUTCOMES

MANDALAS
YOU CAN
COLOUR OR
SHADE IN

"There are only two ways to live your life.
One is as though nothing is a miracle.
The other is as everything is a miracle."
- Albert Einstein

ENVIRONMENTAL

Your Environmental World is everything around you. It gives context to your life. What's context exactly? That's the time, place and era in which anything happens, along with the interaction with the people in it. Nothing exists in isolation and all has relativity to other events and outcomes, just ask Einstein!

Where and when life takes place is part of your contextual reality. This is a good place to start your journey, but not necessarily. You can come back to this area at another point, but whenever you look at the Environment, it's a vital World, one which you cannot ignore.

Your environment would be considered a base-level need, a safety and security requirement. When you live in a dangerous environment and your survival is at risk, little else can be focused on. Here's a question for you; do you take your spaces for granted? Often, it's only when the storm hits, you appreciate those calm days. Your environment provides security and safety, but like all things, it's dynamic and changing.

Your environment also shapes your human culture and impacts the way you interact with those around you. While culture is a social-force (Social World), one that gives you social norms for interactions. It's through your environment, in which culture is created.

For example, look at the culture of the Arctic Inuit. It's shaped by their cold climate, icy landscapes and the resources they can access, therefore this impacts the sports they play, customs they have and the clothing they wear. These will be different to the people of Tropical Polynesia, where they have the same basic needs, but due to their much warmer habitat, they fulfill them very differently. This is how diverse cultures emerge. Climate and place have influenced your culture greatly.

YOUR ENVIRONMENT

YOUR CULTURE

YOU

Place is important, it binds you to the planet and impacts you in many ways. You humans have shaped and changed your surroundings more than any other species.

In the past, humans lived in more harmony with their environments, but that has changed. Today, the human impact is significant and it is increasingly negative. While the collective challenge is large, you can shape and influence your own environment in a positive and sustainable way! If there is one thing I know for sure, you, and all of us, must respect the environments which we live.

If you are fortunate enough to live in a safe and healthy environment, you're off to a good start, but that's just the beginning.

You do have influence, at least in part, where you spend some of your time. You can also create more harmony in the spaces around you. Think about the places and spaces of importance to you and how they make you feel?

THE 2ND BIGGEST ENVIRONMENTAL CHANGER?
THE BEAVER,
THROUGH ITS TIRELESS CUTTING-DOWN OF TREES AND DAMMING RIVERS, CAUSING MAJOR CHANGES TO LANDSCAPES.

ENVIRONMENTAL

Indigenous people all over the world share a deep, spiritual connection to place. They collectively understand the need to preserve the natural world for future generations. As stewards of the planet for thousands of years, you can incorporate their understanding through developing 'Respect of Place'.

The Maori people of Aotearoa New Zealand have a word which highlights how many indigenous populations connect with their environments, it's called; 'whakapapa'.

Whakapapa is both a deep connection to land and the roots of one's ancestry. It's a cultural construct that links all known and unknown phenomena in the earthly and spiritual worlds. It maps relationships so that mythology, history, knowledge, custom, philosophies and spiritualities are organized, preserved and transmitted from one generation to the next (The Encyclopedia of New Zealand).

Maori, First Nations, Aboriginals, Indigenous people all over the world can teach us all about developing more respect for place. Planet Earth is diverse, exciting and has never-ending possibilities to explore. Living a fulfilling life is also about connecting with your environment; away from the man-made world and into the natural-made planet. There's no need to climb a mountain; simply go for a walk in a local park, beach, or forest and take it in.

ALL YOUR 8 WORLDS INTERACT WITH EACH OTHER - NONE LIVE IN ISOLATION. 'WHAKAPAPA' ALSO SHOWS HOW ENVIRONMENT, SPIRITUALITY, SOCIAL & INTIMATE WORLDS UNITE

It's not just indigenous populations which have known of the importance of connecting with nature. "One of the first conditions of happiness is that the link between man and nature shall not be broken." (Leo Tolstoy). He, like many others before you, has seen the great value through maintaining a connection with nature. Being outside (except in extreme conditions) has many benefits, it improves your immune system, decreases stress, sparks creativity and increases the likelihood of awe(some) moments. Just making more time to be outside in "green" spaces will do you good (just remember sunscreen).

Your environment is also the base of developing a sense of awe and adventure. This is what makes life more fulfilling and enjoyable. 'Adventure' is defined by you, it doesn't have to be outside, but it does have to be somehow new and exciting (for you) to be an authentic one. Creating more adventure in your life, leads to inspiration and the creation of moments and memories that are the essence of a Great Life.

A sense of safety and security is an integral part of this world. Although that may seem contrary to seeking more adventure,.this isn't the case. Ask a professional skydiver, they'll likely say that the most dangerous thing was their drive to the airport. Jumping out of a plane has risks, but these have been minimized by managing responses (training and practice); and, managing their responses to their environments (safety equipment / experience). It's not about creating danger, it's about exerting control over your surroundings, in a positive way, where you can thrive.

It's about creating places where you can spend quality time with yourself and those around you. A tree is only as strong as its roots. Your roots grow here, in this place, be sure you cultivate and feed the environment in which they develop.

ENVIRONMENTAL

MY SPACES & PLACES

MY PERSONAL SPACE NEEDS

CREATE HARMONIOUS SPACES INDOORS

HOW I CAN CARE FOR THE NATURAL ENVIRONMENT

HOW CAN I SPEND MORE TIME OUTSIDE IN NATURE?

SPENDING TIME OUTSIDE, IN NATURAL AREAS (SAFE & UNPOLLUTED) IS GREAT FOR BOTH MIND & BODY - PARK, BEACH, FOREST OR LAKE. CONNECTING WITH NATURE REDUCES STRESS, INCREASES CREATIVITY & BENEFITS THE WELLBEING OF ALL GREAT APES!

MY SAFE SPACES

YOUR LIFE HAPPENS IN THE PLACES AROUND YOU.
IT'S WHERE IT UNFOLDS. YOU CAN HAVE A DIRECT IMPACT ON YOUR SPACES &
WHERE YOU CHOOSE TO SPEND YOUR TIME.
YOUR MEMORIES & YOUR PLACE IN THE WORLD LIVE RIGHT HERE.

THE PLACES I CAN BE MYSELF

THE PLACES I GO TO UNWIND

THE SPECIAL PLACES FROM MY PAST

THE SPACES AND PLACES I LOVE

WHERE IS YOUR SPECIAL PLACE? SOMEWHERE, ANYWHERE YOU CAN BE
ALONE & FEEL SAFE, TO THINK & REFLECT.
NO NEED TO WRITE IT DOWN, JUST PICTURE THAT PLACE.
IF YOU DON'T HAVE SUCH A PLACE, FIND SUCH A PLACE.

"The Art of Life is a constant re-adjustment to our surroundings."
- Okakura Kakuuzo (Japanese Scholar)

MY OUTDOOR SEASONS
MY SEASONAL OUTSIDE ACTIVITIES & JOYS

"Earth and sky, woods and fields, lakes and rivers, the mountain and the sea are excellent schoolmasters and teach some of us more than we can ever learn from books. "
- Sir John Lubbock (Politician, Philanthropist, Scientist)

MY SUMMER   MY SPRING

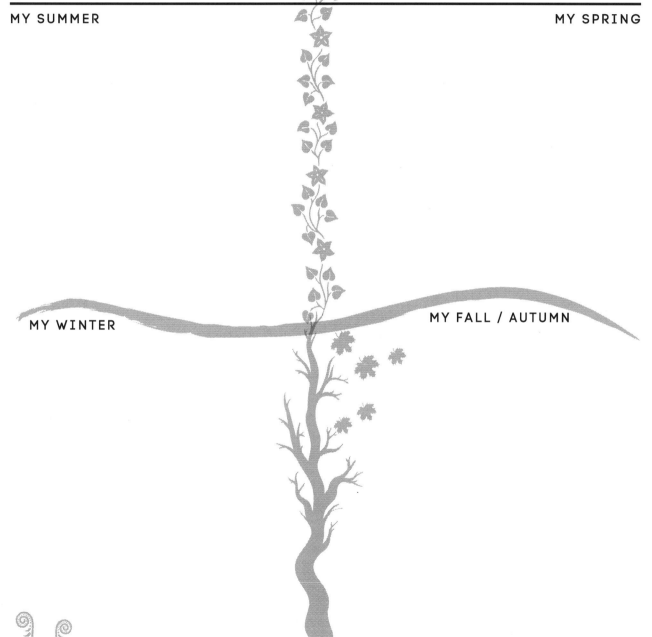

MY WINTER   MY FALL / AUTUMN

"I've found that there is always some beauty left - in Nature, Sunshine, Freedom, in Yourself, these can all help you."
- Anne Frank (Diary of Anne Frank - An Inspiration for ALL of us)

MY INDOOR TASTES

YOUR INSIDE LIVING SPACES IMPACT YOUR WELLBEING, MOODS, HABITS & EMOTIONS - CREATE YOUR SPACE WHERE YOU FEEL COMFORTABLE, INSPIRED & CAN SPEND QUALITY TIME.

MY INDOOR LIFE

MY LIVING SPACE   MY WORK SPACE

MY CLEANLINESS

MY ORGANIZATION

MY MOMENTOS

MY COLOURS / PATTERNS

MY COMFORT

MY NEEDS

"Science is organized knowledge. Wisdom is organized life."
- Immanuel Kant (German Philosopher)

MY CULTURE

YOUR ENVIRONMENT DICTATES YOUR CULTURE. ALTHOUGH YOUR CULTURE IS
PASSED ON TO YOU FROM THOSE AROUND YOU (SOCIAL),
BY UNDERSTANDING YOUR OWN CULTURAL IMPACTS, YOU BETTER UNDERSTAND
YOURSELF & YOUR REACTIONS TO THOSE AROUND YOU.

WHERE AM I FROM?

WHAT CULTURAL GROUPS DO I IDENTIFY?

HOW IS MY CULTURAL BACKGROUND IMPORTANT TO ME?

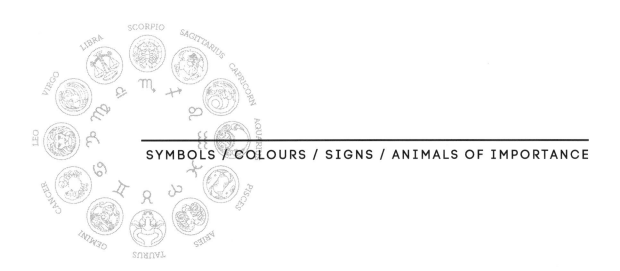

SYMBOLS / COLOURS / SIGNS / ANIMALS OF IMPORTANCE

"We may have different religions, different languages, different
coloured skin, but we all belong to one Human Race."
- Kofi Annan (Former UN Secretary General)

MY PLACES OF MEANING

THE PLACES YOU SPEND YOUR TIME IMPACT YOUR WELLBEING. CONNECTING TO PLACES & KNOWING YOUR PLACES OF MEANING GIVE YOU A PLACE TO BELONG. CREATE YOUR MEANINGFUL SPACES.

WHERE ARE MY SPACES AND PLACES OF SIGNIFICANCE?

HOW IS PLACE IMPORTANT TO ME?

MY COUNTRY / REGION WHERE I FEEL I MOST BELONG.

EXAMPLE

HOW CAN I CREATE MORE CONNECTION WITH PLACE?

DEVELOP CONNECTION WITH PLACE:
- SLOW DOWN - TAKE IT IN
- STAY CURIOUS
- EXPLORE WITH ALL YOUR SENSES
- LEARN THE HISTORY / STORIES
- EXAMINE THE DETAILS (THE SMALL THINGS)
- STAY MINDFUL
- UNDERSTAND WHY IT IS IMPORTANT FOR YOU?
- RESPECT THE MANY PEOPLE WHO HAVE COME BEFORE, YET STAND IN THE SAME PLACE

WHEN I LOOK INTO THE VASTNESS OF THE STARS....?
HOW DO YOU FEEL WHEN YOU LOOK UP ON A CLEAR STARRY NIGHT?

"Some people look for a beautiful place,
others make a place beautiful."
- Hazrat Inayot Khan (Teacher - Founder of the Sufi Order)

MT. EVEREST IS EARTH'S HIGHEST PEAK;

IT'S A PLACE OF GREAT MEANING TO MANY WHO LIE IN HER SHADOW.
CROWNING THE WORLD AT;

8, 848 M

ABOVE SEA LEVEL
(29,029 FT)

IN NEPALESE
SHE IS
"SAGARMATHA"

"GODESS OF THE SKY"

सगरमाथा

IN TIBETAN
HER NAME IS
"CHOMOLUNGMA"

"GODESS MOTHER OF THE
WORLD."

ཇོ་མོ་གླང་ང་མ

"It is not the mountain we conquer
but ourselves."

- Sir Edmund Hillary

ONE MIGHTY
MOUNTAIN -
MANY
PERSPECTIVES.

"EVEREST"
IS NAMED AFTER
SIR GEORGE EVEREST
A BRITISH SURVEYOR.
NOT WANTING THE
HONOUR, HE WOULD
HAVE LIKED IT TO HAVE
A LOCAL NAME...

HILLARY WAS THE FIRST PERSON TO CLIMB THE WORLD'S HIGHEST MOUNTAIN
PEAK IN 1953. ALONG WITH NEPALESE SHERPA, SIR TENZING NORGAY. THEIR
LEGACIES CONTINUE UNTIL TODAY.

MY PERFECT SPACE

USE THIS SPACE TO CREATE YOUR IDEAL / PERFECT SPACE
INDOOR - OUTDOOR - BOTH - WHAT MATTERS TO YOU?

CR∞ MY ADVENTURE

'ADVENTURE' FROM LATIN; "ABOUT TO HAPPEN", SO ADVENTURE IS; "NOT KNOWING WHAT IS ABOUT TO HAPPEN". GETTING OUTSIDE YOUR USUAL ENVIRONMENT, CHALLENGE & TRYING SOMETHING NEW OR DIFFERENT.

CHALLENGE, EXPLORING THE NEW, EXPANDING MY HORIZONS
WHAT DO I WANT TO LEARN / GROW / DEVELOP?

WHAT NEED AM I TRYING TO FULFILL?
WHY?

AM I WILLING TO STEP OUTSIDE MY COMFORT ZONE?
WHAT WILL BE MY ROAD BLOCKS & BARRIERS TO SUCCESS?

NEW ADVENTURE

⚠ WEIGH UP YOUR RISKS
SEE "MY RISKS" PG87

"BE PREPARED" - BADEN POWELL

FROM THE FOUNDER OF THE SCOUT MOVEMENT - ADVICE AS BASIC, AS IT'S TRUE

AM I PREPARED?

DO I NEED THE ADVICE / GUIDANCE / INSTRUCTION?

WHAT TOOLS / SKILLS / MATERIALS WILL I REQUIRE?

ANTICIPATION FROM LATIN "ANTE" - 'BEFORE' & "CAPERE" - 'TAKE'

YOUR FEELINGS BEFORE THE EVENT.

WHAT MINDSET / ATTITUDE WILL I NEED?

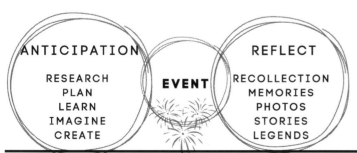

ANTICIPATION
RESEARCH
PLAN
LEARN
IMAGINE
CREATE

EVENT

REFLECT
RECOLLECTION
MEMORIES
PHOTOS
STORIES
LEGENDS

SOME EVENTS ARE BIGGER THAN THEMSELVES. SEE "MY EXPECTATIONS"

ANTICIPATION & REFLECTION ARE OFTEN MORE IMPORTANT & TAKE UP MORE TIME THAN THE EVENT ITSELF. THINK ABOUT THE EXCITEMENT YOU FEEL WHEN LOOKING FORWARD TO SOMETHING, AWAITING A BIG EVENT, AS WELL AS THE BONDS & STORIES IT CREATES AFTERWARDS.

MY ADVENTURE CALANDAR

YOU DON'T NEED TO CLIMB A REAL MOUNTAIN. IT'S A METAPHOR.
AN ADVENTURE IS YOUR OWN WAY OF EXPLORING THE NEW, DIFFERENT,
OR THE UNKNOWN - IN THE WORLD AROUND YOU.

JANUARY	FEBRUARY	MARCH
APRIL	MAY	JUNE
JULY	AUGUST	SEPTEMBER
OCTOBER	NOVEMBER	DECEMBER

"Because in the end. You won't remember the time you spent
working in the office or mowing the lawn.
Climb that goddamn mountain." - Jack Kerouac (Writer)

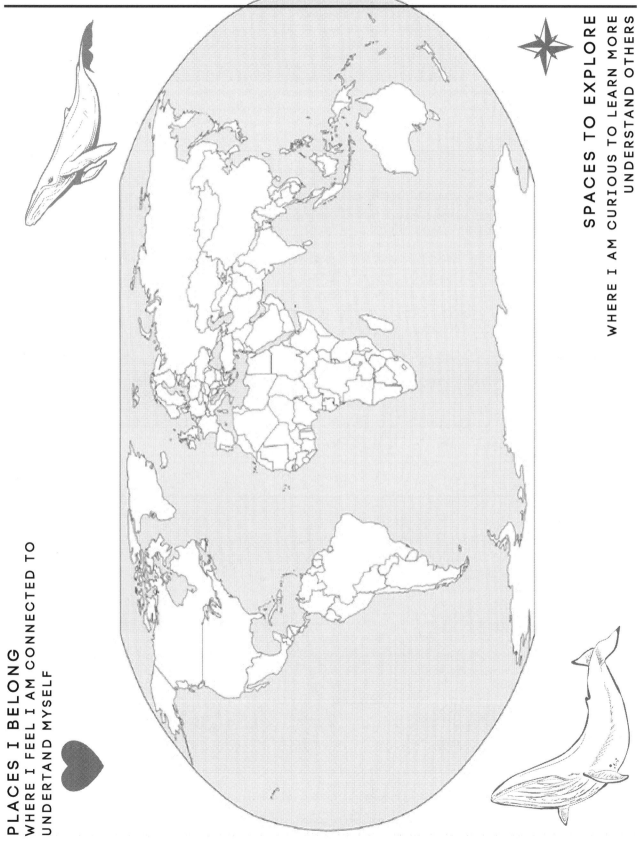

SPACES TO EXPLORE

WHERE I AM CURIOUS TO LEARN MORE UNDERSTAND OTHERS

PLACES I BELONG

WHERE I FEEL I AM CONNECTED TO UNDERTAND MYSELF

MY FOUR ELEMENTS

MY ELEMENTS - CONNECTING TO NATURE

FIRE - MY SPARK
SUNSHINE, WARMTH, MOTIVATION
WHAT CREATES MY FIRE WITHIN?
(PASSIONS & MOTIVATIONS)

WATER - MY SPLASH
ANIMALS, PLANTS, MOVEMENT & GROWTH
WHERE DO I LOOK FOR CHANCES FOR GROWTH?

"Everybody needs beauty as well as bread, places to play in and pray in, where nature may heal and give strength to body and soul."
- John Muir (Botanist, Writer, "Father of US National Parks")

AIR - MY BREATH
CLEAN AIR, WIND, ATMOSPHERE
WHERE DO I FIND CALM & PEACE?

EARTH - MY ROCK
SECURITY, PLACE & ROOTS
WHERE DO I FEEL MOST SECURE?

FOR INDIGENOUS PEOPLE AROUND THE WORLD - PLACE IS SACRED,
IT'S A CONNECTION TO THE EARTH & TO ANCESTORS PAST.

"We are just visitors to this time, this place. we are just passing through. our purpose here is to observe, to learn, to grow and to love... and then we return home."
- Australian Aboriginal Proverb

47

MY ADAPTATION

"Intelligence is the ability to adapt to change." - Stephen Hawking

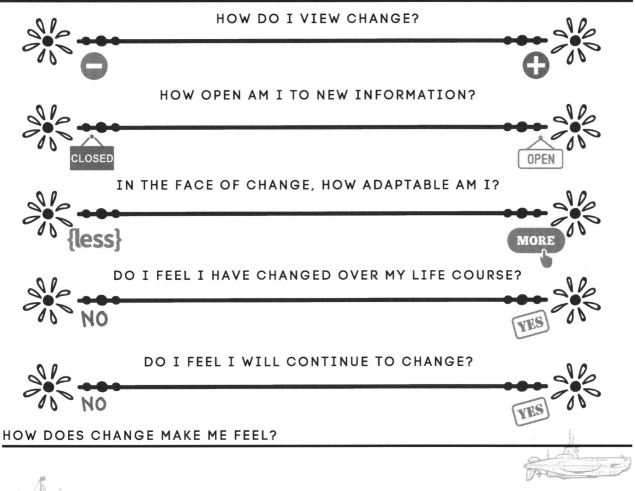

HOW DO I VIEW CHANGE?

−   +

HOW OPEN AM I TO NEW INFORMATION?

CLOSED   OPEN

IN THE FACE OF CHANGE, HOW ADAPTABLE AM I?

{less}   MORE

DO I FEEL I HAVE CHANGED OVER MY LIFE COURSE?

NO   YES

DO I FEEL I WILL CONTINUE TO CHANGE?

NO   YES

HOW DOES CHANGE MAKE ME FEEL?

HOW DO I BEST ADAPT TO CHANGE?

HAVING A SOUND MISSION / VALUES WILL OFFER STABILITY IN THE FACE OF CHANGE - EVEN AS THESE MAY ADAPT OVER TIME, THEY OFFER AN ANCHOR IN THE MOVING WAVES.

- LET GO OF REGRET (YOU CAN'T CHANGE THE PAST)
- WRITE IT DOWN (PROCESS THE CHANGE)
- KEEP PLANS FLEXIBLE (ADAPT TO NEW REALITIES)
- UNDERSTAND THERE ARE THINGS WITHIN / OUTSIDE YOUR CONTROL
- CHANGE YOUR PERSPECTIVE / REACTION (SEE CHANGE AS NEW OPPORTUNITIES)

"Change is the law of life and those who only look to the past and present are sure to miss the future."
- John F. Kennedy (35th President of the United States)

MY NEEDS

"NEEDS" = 'OF NECESSITY' (FOR LIFE)
THE "NEEDS" MODEL SUGGESTS LOWER, BASIC NEEDS REQUIRE FULFILLMENT
BEFORE HIGHER ONES CAN BE ATTAINED.

LOWER LEVEL NEEDS FULFILLED BEFORE HIGHER

SELF-ACTUALIZATION
ADVANCING ONE'S FULL POTENTIAL, PERSONAL
DEVELOPMENT AND CREATIVITY

ESTEEM NEEDS
RESPECT, SELF-ESTEEM, STATUS,
RECOGNITION, FREEDOM

LOVE & BELONGING NEEDS
FRIENDSHIP, INTIMACY, FAMILY, SOCIAL CONNECTION

SAFETY NEEDS
PERSONAL /FAMILY SECURITY, EMPLOYMENT, RESOURCES,
HEALTH, PROPERTY

PHYSIOLOGICAL NEEDS
AIR, WATER, FOOD, SHELTER, CLOTHING, SLEEP

BASED ON PSYCHOLOGY PROFESSOR - ABRAHAM MASLOW'S
MOTIVATIONAL THEORY- HIERARCHY OF NEEDS

MY UNFULFILLED NEEDS

MY ACTIONS TO HIGHER NEEDS

∞ REAL LIFE DOES NOT WORK IN TRIANGLES, NOR STRAIGHT LINES.
THIS MODEL HIGHLIGHTS THE IMPORTANCE OF LOOKING AFTER YOUR MOST BASIC (BASE)
EXAMPLE NEEDS - THOSE BEING YOUR PHYSICAL SELF (BODY) & THE ENVIRONMENT YOU LIVE IN.

"One of the basic needs of every human being is the need to be
loved, to have our wishes and feelings taken seriously, to be validated
as people who matter." - Harold S. Kushner (American Rabbi, Author)

PHYSICAL

"I've missed more than 9000 shots in my career.
I've lost almost 300 games. 26 times, I've been
trusted to take the game winning shot and missed.
I've failed over and over and over again in my life.
And that is why I succeed."
- Michael Jordan

PHYSICAL

You live in your Body. That may seem obvious, but your body is probably not always given the respect it deserves. Your body is what you use to interact with the physical world, the people around you and the environment in which you live.

The Physical World, along with your environment, are base security and safety needs. Take a look at Maslow's famous 'Hierarchy of Needs" on the preceding page. Like the environment, if your physical health is suffering, it impacts all other areas of your life. If you're physically sick, or have a health issue, it often becomes the center of attention, as it should be, you need to focus on healing.

In today's world, while your life may be less physically demanding than in the past; your 21st century lifestyle is probably making you sicker, rather than healthier. Your 'easier' life has also naturally made it more sedentary. Add in a cheap, high-calorie, highly-processed diet and the result; an epidemic of lifestyle diseases and debilitating conditions. These are now starting to reduce the quality of life of a generation. Life length might still be expanding, but that does not mean Quality of Life years is also increasing.

You don't have to be perfect, but you do have to be kind to your body. That's if you want it to be pain-free, disease-free and healthy; both in body and mind. What you do with your body now, and what you put in your body everyday, impacts your whole life, not just your physical world. Do you stop and think about the consequences of this?

You may fear terrorism, war, disaster, but the statistics show, very clearly, it's your lifestyle; what you eat, drink and how you move, which will likely get the better of you. It's about understanding the truth, not falling for the fear.

"Your Body is your Temple", as the saying goes. It's through your physical body in which your mind and soul engage with the physical earth and the environment in which we all live and share. Are you happy with how you are treating your "Temple"?

"Movement is the Best Medicine". There are few things better you can do for yourself than regularly moving your body and exerting stress on your muscles in the process. Sweat, through movement is good for you. There's now an abundance of research that shows regular movement will help you live longer, feel better, fight disease and improve your quality of life.

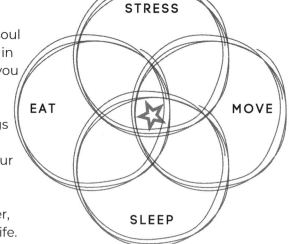

"You are what you Eat", this holds true. Your body and all its parts require nutrition to function and remain at optimal levels to fight the 'bad guys', be that disease, infection or inflammation. As important as movement, is what you feed your temple, that's your daily medicine.

"Sleep your way to Success", all creatures Great and small need their rest. In some way shape or form, 'life' needs time for restoration. Sleep is that time for humans. Getting enough quality sleep will help you decrease stress, build muscle and be mentally sharper. Good health starts and ends with getting enough sleep.

PHYSICAL

You aren't given an owners manual for your body, but there is ever-increasing research that backs up the fundamentals of good human health. This is a world you have control over, direct control! By incorporating the collective human knowledge on what's good for you, if you're fortunate to have a functioning body and the ability to choose what you put in it, you can make real changes here. Not all at once, but in small steps, and this will influence all your worlds in amazing ways.

In this section, you're going to examine the very basics about what you need to know about good physical health and how you can incorporate it directly into your daily life. It's why the holistic approach works, the focus is not just on physiological muscle movements and what food you eat, but also examining the motivation that keeps you going with it, habits, routines, connecting with others; making good physical health an essential part of your full life and an intentional one.

It's about developing a Strong Body, not a slim body or a muscular physique, but strength. You will feel confident in a stronger body, you will BE stronger. Starting small with little increments is the way to progress.

It's about how you move and ensuring you are having fun. If you don't find a way to move that you enjoy, you'll never keep with it. Moving is your body's default, it wants you to get off the sofa!

The food you eat everyday matters. Nutrition is important. A lot of highly processed foods may be giving you the calories, but not the nutrients you require. The human body needs calories (energy) and nutrients (repair & grow) to have a fully functioning machine. Healthy eating is not calorie counting, it's about Conscious Eating.

You aren't just a victim of your genes, you can impact your physical future and create good health. Good long-term health habits will positively impact your whole life and life course. It's that fundamental! The choices you make now, in this world. will impact your future health. So if your aim is 'Quality of Life', take action!

Your Physical World is something that you can exert control over, if you choose. Make it fun and motivating by incorporating new learning, challenges and personal growth. Ready, Set...

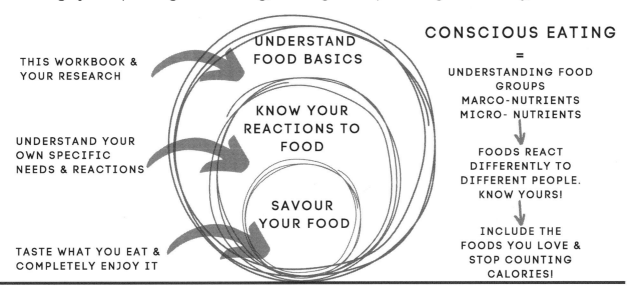

THIS WORKBOOK & YOUR RESEARCH

UNDERSTAND YOUR OWN SPECIFIC NEEDS & REACTIONS

TASTE WHAT YOU EAT & COMPLETELY ENJOY IT

UNDERSTAND FOOD BASICS

KNOW YOUR REACTIONS TO FOOD

SAVOUR YOUR FOOD

CONSCIOUS EATING
=
UNDERSTANDING FOOD GROUPS
MARCO-NUTRIENTS
MICRO- NUTRIENTS

FOODS REACT DIFFERENTLY TO DIFFERENT PEOPLE. KNOW YOURS!

INCLUDE THE FOODS YOU LOVE & STOP COUNTING CALORIES!

PHYSICAL

MY STRONG & HEALTHY BODY

KEY HEALTH INDICATORS

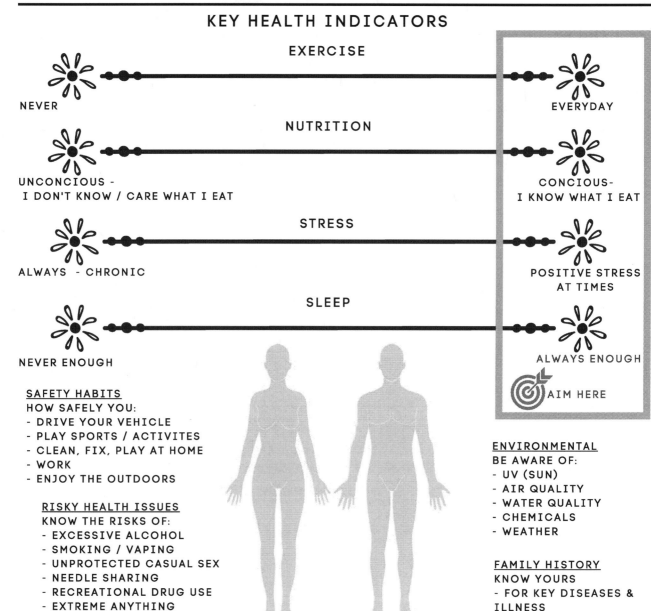

EXERCISE

NEVER — EVERYDAY

NUTRITION

UNCONCIOUS -
I DON'T KNOW / CARE WHAT I EAT — CONCIOUS-
I KNOW WHAT I EAT

STRESS

ALWAYS - CHRONIC — POSITIVE STRESS
AT TIMES

SLEEP

NEVER ENOUGH — ALWAYS ENOUGH
AIM HERE

SAFETY HABITS
HOW SAFELY YOU:
- DRIVE YOUR VEHICLE
- PLAY SPORTS / ACTIVITES
- CLEAN, FIX, PLAY AT HOME
- WORK
- ENJOY THE OUTDOORS

RISKY HEALTH ISSUES
KNOW THE RISKS OF:
- EXCESSIVE ALCOHOL
- SMOKING / VAPING
- UNPROTECTED CASUAL SEX
- NEEDLE SHARING
- RECREATIONAL DRUG USE
- EXTREME ANYTHING

ENVIRONMENTAL
BE AWARE OF:
- UV (SUN)
- AIR QUALITY
- WATER QUALITY
- CHEMICALS
- WEATHER

FAMILY HISTORY
KNOW YOURS
- FOR KEY DISEASES &
ILLNESS

MY FOCUS AREAS

MY MEDICAL CHECK-UPS:

DOCTOR

DENTIST

SPECIALIST

"The body is a house of God. That is why it's said
'Know Thyself'." - Ancient Egyptian Proverb

MY FOOD

MY HEALTHY EATING GUIDELINES

MY FOCUS FOODS - SHOPPING LIST

80%

80%
GOOD,
WHOLESOME FOOD

20% (OR LESS)- TREATS & CHEATS

CHECKLIST
- CONSCIOUS EATING
- WHOLE FOODS
- VARIETY - COLOURS
- FIBER-RICH
- VEGETABLES & FRUIT
- LEGUMES & PULSES (BEANS)
- NUTS & SEEDS
- HEALTHY FATS (OLIVE OIL)
- GUT-FRIENDLY FOODS
- HIGH PROTEIN
- NUTRIENT-DENSE
- LOW SUGAR
- LOW SALT

AVOID HIGHLY-PROCESSED
MEATS & CARBS
AVOID TRANS-FAT
AVOID DEEP-FRIED
REDUCE SIMPLE CARBS

YOU HAVE TO ENJOY LIFE & INCORPORATE THE FOODS YOU LOVE
USE THESE AS TREATS & REWARDS - NOT EVERYDAY SNACK ITEMS.

20% - MY TREATS

THESE ARE ALL GUIDELINES ONLY
- UNDERSTAND YOUR NUTRITION REQUIREMENTS

"Take care of your body, it's the only place you have to live."
- Jim Rohn (Author, Entrepreneur, Motivational Speaker)

MACRO = BIG

YOU NEED THESE TO SURVIVE - IN LARGE AMOUNTS
YOUR CALORIES TO SURVIVE COME FROM HERE

MY MACRO-NUTRIENTS

WATER

WHY? - YOU NEED THIS FOR SURVIVAL
MORE THAN FOOD

WATCH YOUR POP! (& YOUR FRAPPACINO)
A 355ML CAN OF COKE / PEPSI HAS
ALMOST 10 TEASPOONS OF PURE SUGAR!
SUGAR IS A SIMPLE CARB - SEE BELOW

BASED ON RECOMMENDATIONS FROM THE WORLD HEALTH
ORGANIZATION (WHO) & US DIETERY GUIDELINES 2020-2025

WATER
CLEAN FRESH
WATER IS BEST

GUIDELINES

8 GLASSES OR
1.8-2 LITERS PER DAY
OR, WHEN THIRSTY

FAT (FATTY ACIDS)

WHY? - YOU NEED FAT;
IT'S AN ENERGY SOURCE;
ABSORBS MINERALS;
REGULATES DIGESTION;
BODY NEEDS ESSENTIAL
FATTY ACIDS FROM FOOD.

{less}

DEEP FRIED;
PROCESSED MEATS & CARBS;
MARGARINES & HYDROGENERATED VEGETABLE OIL
HEAVY SAUCES & DRESSINGS.

WORSE FATS

SATURATED FAT
TRANS FATS
LOW-DENSITY LIPO-
PROTEIN (LDL)
THE 'NOT SO GOOD'
CHOLESTEROL

BETTER FATS

UNSATURATED FAT
MONO & POLY
ESSENTIAL FATTY ACIDS
OMEGA 3 & 6
YOU NEED TO GET THESE
FROM FOOD
GOOD CHOLESTEROL
(HDL)

OLIVE / CANOLA OILS
AVOCADO
FATTY FISH
SEEDS
DAIRY
NUTS
EGGS
BEANS
SOY
OLIVES
TOFU
LEAN MEAT

20 - 35%

PROTEIN (AMINO ACIDS)

WHY? BUILDING BLOCKS,
MUSCLE REPAIR, ENERGY,
STRENGTH, RESISTANCE &
ENDURANCE.

20 AMINO ACIDS MAKE
PROTEIN.
YOUR BODY MAKES 11
YOU NEED - 9 ESSENTIAL
AMINO ACIDS FROM YOUR
DIET.

**INCOMPLETE
PROTEIN**
NOT ALL 9 ESSENTIALS
SO USE FOOD
COMBINATIONS

GRAINS + LEGUMES
RICE & BEANS
NUTS/SEEDS + LEGUMES
HUMMUS & PITA

**COMPLETE
PROTEIN**
ALL 9 ESSENTIALS
MEAT
EGGS
DAIRY
SOY
QUINOA
CHIA / HEMPSEED

MEAT
DAIRY
FISH
EGGS
BEANS
LENTILS
LEGUMES
NUTS
GRAINS
SEEDS
INSECTS

 REDUCE YOUR CARBON FOOTPRINT BY
EATING LESS MEAT - SMART PROTEIN SWAPS

MIX IT UP

15 - 35%

CARBOHYDRATES (CARBS)

WHY? ENERGY SOURCE,
NUTRIENTS & DIGESTION

THERE ARE 3 PARTS
TO CARBOHYDRATES
• FIBRE - COMPLEX
• STARCH - COMPLEX
• SUGAR - SIMPLE

THE DIFFERENCE
IS VERY IMPORTANT!

⚠ THIS IS THE WESTERN
DIETS BIGGEST PROBLEM

SIMPLE CARBS
SOURCE OF ENERGY -
SPIKES BLOOD SUGAR
BREAKS-DOWN QUICKLY
MORE HUNGER PAINS
IF NOT USED- STORED
AS BODY FAT
LITTLE NUTRITION
POORER QUALITY
ENERGY

{less}

COMPLEX CARBS
KEEPS YOU FEELING
FULLER - LONGER
BREAKS DOWN SLOWER
FULL OF NUTRIENTS
AIDS DIGESTION/
ABSORBTION
AIDS REGULAR BOWEL
MOVEMENTS

MORE

VEGETABLES
FRUIT
WHOLE GRAINS
RICE
QUINOA
COUSCOUS
NUTS
BEANS
PULSES
LENTILS

45 - 65%
CUSTOMIZE TO YOUR NEEDS

"Let food be thy medicine and medicine be thy food."
- Hippocrates (Father of Modern Western Medicine)

MY MICRO-NUTRIENTS

MICRO = SMALL   YOU NEED THESE TO RUN YOUR BODY - EACH IN A SMALL AMOUNT
A HEALTHY FULLY-FUNCTIONING BODY NEEDS THESE TO THRIVE

BASIC VITAMINS / MINERALS FOR HUMAN FUNCTION

VITAMINS

A,
B1, B2, B3, B5,
B6, B7, B9, B12,
C,
D,
E
K

MINERALS

CALCIUM, PHOSPHORUS,
SODIUM, CHLORIDE,
MANGANESE, SELENIUM,
IRON, MAGNESIUM,
POTASSIUM, ZINC,
COPPER, MOLYDENUM,
IODINE, CHROMIUM...

ANTIOXIDANTS

ANTI-OXIDANTS ARE
COMPOUNDS WHICH
INHIBIT (FIGHT)
OXIDATION.
OXIDATION IS BAD FOR
YOUR BODY AS IT CAUSES
FREE-RADICALS, FREE-
RADICALS ARE UNSTABLE
ATOMS WHICH DAMAGE
YOUR BODY.

HOW I CAN INCORPORATE MY MICRO-NUTRIENTS?

ANTIOXIDANT RICH FOODS - LOTS OF COLOURS & VARIETY
- **RED-BLUE** - BERRIES, GRAPES, APPLES, TOMATOES, BEETS, WINE
- **GREEN** - DARK LEAFY GREENS, LIMES, BROCOLI, AVACADO, TEA
- **ORANGE** - CARROT, SWEET POTATO, SQUASH, ROOT VEGE, MANGO
- **YELLOW** - LEMONS, BANANA, PINEAPPLE, MELON, BELL PEPPERS
- **BROWN** - WHOLE GRAINS, RICE, NUTS, COFFEE, SEEDS, CHOCOLATE (DARK)
- **WHITE** - ONIONS, GARLIC, LEEKS, CAULIFLOWER, FISH, SHELLFISH, TEA
IT'S ABOUT BALANCE - TOO MUCH OF ANY OF THESE HAS THE EXACT OPPOSITE EFFECT!

COFFEE
FRESH IS BEST!
LIGHTER ROAST
= MORE
ANTIOXIDANTS &
MORE CAFFEINE!

TEA
SKIP THE MILK
ADD VITAMIN. C
(LEMON)

NO CAFFEINE
TRY HERBAL
MINT, GINGER,
C(H)AMOMILE
...

NOT TOO
HOT!
LET IT
COOL.

ADD MICRONUTRIENTS NATURALLY
WANT FLAVOUR & SPICE? TRY THESE:

CINNAMON
PAPRIKA
CUMIN
BLACK PEPPER
TUMERIC
CHILLI
ROSEMARY
THYME
OREGANO
BASIL
CILANTRO / CORRIANDER
CLOVES
GARLIC
GINGER
LEMONGRASS
CARDAMOM
NUTMEG
FENNEL
MUSTARD
MINT
LEMON/LIME
DILL
SEA / ROCK SALT

THE BEST WAY TO GET THESE IS THROUGH A BALANCED DIET
RICH IN COLOURS, FLAVOURS, WITH A WHOLE FOODS FOCUS.
VARIETY IS LITERALLY THE SPICES YOU ADD TO LIFE

"Natural forces within us are the true healers of disease."

- Hippocrates

PHYSICIANS STILL TAKE THE 'HIPPOCRATIC OATH' & STILL USE HIS ANCIENT GREEK PRINCIPLES
AS THE BASE FOR ETHICAL MEDICAL PRACTICE. SOME ADVICE IS TIMELESS.

MY DIET

"DIET" = 'WHAT YOU TYPICALLY EAT'.

NOT THE SAME AS "GOING ON A DIET" - WHICH IS TYPICALLY SHORT TERM, HIGHLY RESTRICTIVE, AVOIDING FOOD GROUPS & IT'S OFTEN UNSUSTAINABLE.
UNDERSTANDING YOUR DIET TO CREATE LONG-TERM HEALTHY EATING HABITS & DEVELOPING A HEALTHY RELATIONSHIP WITH FOOD. THIS IS WHAT YOUR DIET SHOULD BE!

MY BIGGEST DIET PROBLEMS
- HUNGER?
- LOTS OF CHEAPER, EASIER, YUMMY, HIGHLY-PROCESSED OPTIONS?
-
-

HOW DO I FEEL ABOUT FOOD?
WHAT HAVE I LEARNT ABOUT MY PAST DIETS

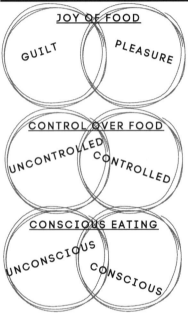

DO NOT FEAR FOOD - DEVELOP A HEALTHY RELATIONSHIP WITH FOOD BY:
- INCORPORATE WHAT YOU ENJOY.
- LEARN ABOUT FOOD (YOU WILL DO THIS HERE, I HOPE).
- KNOW THE IMPORTANCE OF YOUR "POWER SOURCES" & "NUTRIENT SOURCES".
- UNDERSTAND HEALTHY FOOD DOES NOT EQUAL BORING FOOD.
- IT'S ABOUT MAKING SMART ALTERNATIVES & SWITCHES.
- DEVELOP YOUR PALATE (TASTES) - TRY NEW & ADD VARIETY
- ENJOY FOOD TOGETHER WITH OTHERS; SHARE, PREPARE, GATHER, CELEBRATE (WHEN SAFE)
- DEVELOP A BETTER APPRECIATION FOR FOOD (NO NEED TO BECOME A GOURMET CHEF)
- KNOW YOUR FOOD TRIGGERS - LOOK FOR SOLUTIONS & TOOLS

UNDERSTAND YOUR HUNGER - STAY IN THE GREY

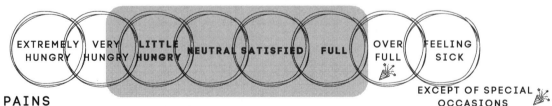

EXCEPT OF SPECIAL OCCASIONS

HUNGER PAINS
- HUNGER. HOW MUCH CONTROL DO YOU HAVE OVER IT? IT'S PARTIALLY CAUSED BY A CHEMICAL "GHRELIN" - IT INCREASES AS THE STOMACH EMPTIES.
- HUNGER DOESN'T MEAN YOU MUST EAT, YOUR BODY WANTS AN EASY ENERGY SOURCE.
- HUNGER IS AS MUCH MENTAL AS IT IS PHYSICAL. YOU LIKELY HAVE PLENTY OF ENERGY STORES. (REMEMBER YOUR EXTRA ENERGY NEEDS DURING MENTAL & PHYSICAL EXERTION)
- INTERMITTENED FASTING - ALLOWING YOUR DIGESTIVE SYSTEM REST (EG. 12-16HRS/DAY) - HAS PROVEN HEALTH BENEFITS (RESEARCH IF THIS COULD BE RIGHT FOR YOU?)

MY GUT

MY GUT HEALTH IS - MY MIND & BODY HEALTH

GUT FEELING - GUT INTUITION - WHY DO YOU FEEL IT IN YOUR GUT? YOUR GUT IS MORE THAN JUST A FOOD PROCESSOR - IT'S HOME TO ITS OWN NERVOUS SYSTEM (ENTERIC) & HAS ITS OWN BRAIN CELLS!

HOW I CAN IMPROVE MY GUT HEALTH?

GUT FLORA

OR "MICROBIOTA" ARE MICRO-ORGANISMS (BACTERIA & FUNGI) THAT LIVE YOUR GUT & DIGESTIVE TRACT. IT'S HOME TO THE MOST DIVERSE & NUMEROUS OF ALL LIVING THINGS IN YOUR BODY.

IMPROVE YOUR GUT HEALTH BY:

- UNDERSTAND WHAT YOU EAT - YOUR GUT FLORA IMPACT YOUR HEALTH IN MANY WAYS
- MOVING YOUR BODY - PROMOTES GUT FLORA GROWTH.
- REDUCING CHRONIC STRESS - TOO MUCH STRESS ALLOWS THE BAD BACTERIA IN.
- GET OUTSIDE - EXPOSURE TO GOOD BACTERIA IN THE NATURAL ENVIRONMENT.
- GET ENOUGH SLEEP - RESTORE TIME FOR ALL YOUR BODY.
- STOP SMOKING - KILLS - UPSETS GUT BACTERIA.
- AVOID UN-NECESSARY ANTIBIOTICS / ANTI-INFLAMMATORIES - THEY CAN KILL BOTH GOOD & BAD GUT BACTERIA - ASK YOUR DOCTOR FOR ADVICE.
- EAT WELL - VARIETY & COLOUR.

MY "GO-TO" GUT- FRIENDLY FOODS?

EATING WELL FOR YOUR GUT
FERMENTED FOODS
WHOLE FOODS
HIGH FIBRE
VARIETY
HERBS/SPICES/COLOURS

DID YOU KNOW?

- YOU HAVE 10X MORE MICROBES IN YOUR GUT THAN HUMAN CELLS IN THE BODY, TRILLIONS.
- 70% OF YOUR IMMUNE SYSTEM IS ACTIVATED BY YOUR GUT.
- YOUR GUT HAS ITS OWN BRAIN & BRAIN CELLS - 100 MILLION OF THEM, GIVE OR TAKE.
- YOUR GUT IS THE GUARDIAN BETWEEN THE OUTSIDE & INSIDE WORLD.
- MUCH OF YOUR SEROTONIN IS PRODUCED IN THE GUT - YOUR "FEEL GOOD" CHEMICAL.
- YOU CAN FEEL IT IN YOUR GUT BECAUSE YOUR GUT CAN FEEL & IMPACT HOW YOU FEEL.

BASED ON RESEARCH & ADVICE BY HARVARD MEDICAL SCHOOL & JOHN HOPKINS UNIVERSITY

MY MEAL PLANNER

WEEK #   GOAL

MONDAY	TUESDAY	WEDNESDAY

THURSDAY	FRIDAY	SATURDAY

SUNDAY	MEAL TIMINGS

USE THIS AS A GUIDE & MIX IT UP

COOKING FOR ONE? OR A FAMILY? FREEZE / REFRIGERATE LEFTOVERS - PORTION OUT OR REIMAGINE INTO FUTURE MEALS - A SIMPLE STIR-FRY CAN BE MADE INTO WRAPS, SALADS, BAKES, BOWLS OR CURRIES.

MY MOMENTS OF STRENGTH

"STRENGTH" - "THE ABILITY TO WITHSTAND FORCE AND PRESSURE"

MY MOMENTS OF STRENGTH

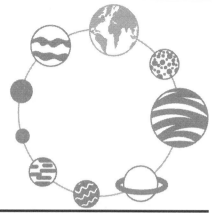

WHY IT MAKES ME STRONG?

MY "GIFTS & TALENTS"   VALUING MY STRENGTHS

HOW CAN I USE MY STRENGTHS TO HELP OTHERS?

"Strength does not come from winning. Your struggles develop your strengths, when you go through hardships and decide not to surrender, that is Strength."
- Mahatma Gandhi (Freedom-fighter, Peace-maker, Teacher & Guru)

MY MOMENTS OF WEAKNESS

"WEAKNESS" - "A PERSON OR THING THAT ONE IS UNABLE TO RESIST OR LIKES EXCESSIVELY."

"Falling down is not Failure. Failure comes when you stay where you have fallen." - Socrates (Ancient Greek Philosopher)

MY MOMENTS OF WEAKNESS

WHY I FEEL WEAK / LACK CONTROL?

MY EXCESSES & EXTREMES

MY STATEGIES

"One of the basic rules of the universe is that nothing is perfect. Perfection simply doesn't exist... without imperfection, neither you nor I would exist."

- Stephen Hawking (Theoretical Physicist & Author)

MY MOVEMENT

MY STRENGTH

EVERYONE, AT EVERY AGE BENEFITS FROM SOME FORM OF RESISTANCE TRAINING - NO WEIGHTS REQUIRED, BODYWEIGHT WORKS!

MY CARDIO

GET YOUR HEART PUMPING & SWEAT, DETOX YOUR BODY & STRENGTHEN YOUR IMMUNE SYSTEM & BONES

MY FLEXIBILITY

EXAMPLE

MIND + BODY - AFTER A WORKOUT, YOUR BODY IS REVITALIZED & STIMULATED. AFTER YOUR COOL DOWN, SIT - BREATHE SLOWLY (4-8-4) & FOCUS -IF YOU STRUGGLE WITH MEDITATION, THIS IS A GREAT TIME TO TRY. FEEL YOUR BODY

IF YOU WANT A BODY THAT IS KIND TO YOU, BE KIND TO IT. GIVE IT A STRETCH; YOGA, PILATES, TAI-CHI, FOAM ROLLER, MASSAGE...

MY FUN / RECOVERY

THE BEST WAY TO STICK WITH EXERCISE IS TO FIND SOMETHING YOU LIKE. MAKE MOVING FUN! SET A CHALLENGE!

MY MOVEMENT WEEKLY PLANNER

MY MOVEMENT GOAL:

WEEKLY GUIDELINES		WHAT - WHERE - WHEN

FLEXIBLITY — 10-15 MINS / DAY / 5 - 7 DAYS

WARM - MOVE - COOL
WARM UP FOR 5 MINS BEFORE;
COOL DOWN AFTERWARDS FOR 5 MINS

- YOGA
- PILATES
- TAI-CHI
- STRETCHING
- FOAM ROLLING
- BALANCE EXERCISES
- POSES / HOLDS

WHY?
IMPROVE JOINTS. BETTER RANGE OF MOTION. RELAX MUSCLES. REGULATE BREATHING. DECREASE STIFFNESS. LESS INJURIES.

RESISTANCE — 30-45 MINS / DAY / 2 / 3 DAYS

- BODYWEIGHT EXERCISES
- FREE-WEIGHTS
- RESISTANCE BANDS
- WEIGHT MACHINES
- CLASSES
- BOXING
- SWISS-BALL
- PADDLE / ROW
- SWIM

WHY?
BUILD MUSCLE. INCREASE BONE DENSITY. CORE STRENGTH. BETTER POSTURE. GREATER CALORIE BURN. UPPER & LOWER BODY STRENGTH & POWER

CARDIO — 20-60 MINS / DAY / 3 /4 DAYS

- CLASSES
- TEAM SPORTS
- HIIT
- SWIM
- BIKE
- RUN / WALK
- ROW / PADDLE
- SKI / BOARD
- RIDE
- CLIMB
- MARTIAL ARTS
- DANCE
- CLEAN / CREATE

WHY?
INCREASING HEART & LUNG HEALTH. REGULATE BLOOD PRESSURE. DECREASE STRESS. DECREASE DISEASE. FEEL BETTER.

MORE TIME — LESS TIME
LESS INTENSE (WALKING) — 30 MINS — MORE INTENSE (SPRINTING)

FUN — HOW CAN I INCORPORATE FUN THINGS I LIKE? — EVERYDAY

WHY?
STICK WITH IT. ENJOY IT LIFELONG.

BASED ON W.H.O. GLOBAL RECOMMENDATIONS FOR GLOBAL PHYSICAL ACTIVITY 2019

BUILD STRENGTH

"It does not matter how slow you go as long as you do not stop."
- Confucius (Ancient Chinese Philosopher, Sage, Teacher & Guru)

"Do the difficult things while they are easy and do the great things while they are small. A journey of a thousand miles must begin with a single step."

- Lao Tzu

老子　"OLD MASTER" - ANCIENT CHINESE PHILOSOPHER & WRITER
SPIRITUAL FOUNDER OF TAOISM

MY WORKOUT SUCCESS

CREATING A HABIT TO MOVE CAN BE HARD! START SMALL. LEARN THE BASICS & KNOW WHAT WILL MOTIVATE YOU. IT'S WORTH THE EFFORT!

WHAT I NEED TO MOVE? WHAT WILL HELP ME MOVE?

MUSIC?
OTHER PEOPLE?
INSTRUCTION?
MORE KNOWLEDGE?
CONFIDENCE?
MOTIVATION?
TIME?

WHAT STOPPING ME? MY MOVEMENT EXCUSES - SOLUTIONS

EXCUSES
- I HAVE NO TIME?
- I DON'T LIKE IT?
- IT HURTS / PAIN?
- NOT SURE WHAT TO DO?
- NO MONEY / RESOURCES?

SOLUTIONS
- I CAN MAKE TIME BY...
- I WILL FIND SOMETHING I LIKE
- I WILL START SMALL - BUILD SLOWLY
- I WILL LEARN / ASK FOR HELP
- I CAN USE FREE RESOURCES - MY BODY

EXAMPLE

SOMETHING NEW I CAN LEARN - MOVE MY BODY IN NEW WAYS

MIXING IT UP

YOUR BODY NEEDS TO BE 'STRESSED' IN NEW & DIFFERENT WAYS - JUST LIKE YOU, YOUR BODY WILL ADAPT AFTER SOME TIME. YOU HAVE TO KEEP THE BAR MOVING - HIGHER OR AT DIFFERENT ANGLES.

MY PROGRESSIVE CHALLENGES

STAGE 1

STAGE 2

STAGE 3

STAGE 4

EXAMPLE

GO FOR A WALK FOR 20MINS - 2-3X WEEK

WALK FOR 30MINS 2X WEEK + 1 BIKE RIDE + STRETCHING

WALK FOR 40MINS 2X WEEK + 2 SWIMS + STRETCHING

WALK/SWIM 40MINS 3X WEEK + BODY WEIGHT EXERCISES + STRETCH

"The pain you feel today will be the strength you have tomorrow."
- On posters in gyms everywhere...

MY STRESSORS

UNDERSTAND THE DIFFERENCE BETWEEN POSITIVE SHORT-TERM
STRESS & NEGATIVE LONG-TERM (CHRONIC) STRESS.

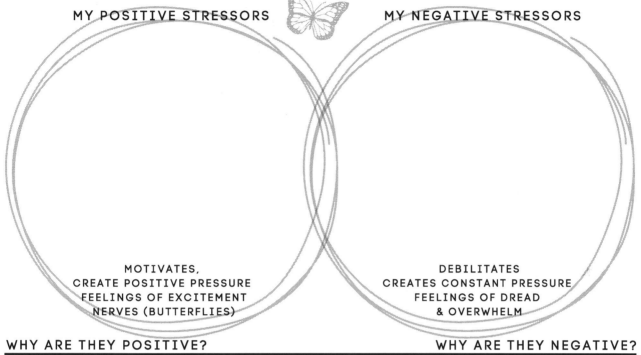

MY POSITIVE STRESSORS

MY NEGATIVE STRESSORS

MOTIVATES,
CREATE POSITIVE PRESSURE
FEELINGS OF EXCITEMENT
NERVES (BUTTERFLIES)

DEBILITATES
CREATES CONSTANT PRESSURE
FEELINGS OF DREAD
& OVERWHELM

WHY ARE THEY POSITIVE?

WHY ARE THEY NEGATIVE?

HOW IT MAKES ME FEEL?

HOW I MANAGE MY NEGATIVE STRESS?

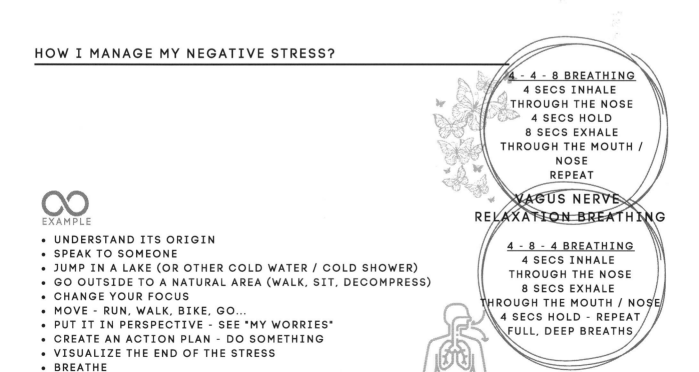

4 - 4 - 8 BREATHING
4 SECS INHALE
THROUGH THE NOSE
4 SECS HOLD
8 SECS EXHALE
THROUGH THE MOUTH /
NOSE
REPEAT

VAGUS NERVE
RELAXATION BREATHING

4 - 8 - 4 BREATHING
4 SECS INHALE
THROUGH THE NOSE
8 SECS EXHALE
THROUGH THE MOUTH / NOSE
4 SECS HOLD - REPEAT
FULL, DEEP BREATHS

∞
EXAMPLE

- UNDERSTAND ITS ORIGIN
- SPEAK TO SOMEONE
- JUMP IN A LAKE (OR OTHER COLD WATER / COLD SHOWER)
- GO OUTSIDE TO A NATURAL AREA (WALK, SIT, DECOMPRESS)
- CHANGE YOUR FOCUS
- MOVE - RUN, WALK, BIKE, GO...
- PUT IT IN PERSPECTIVE - SEE "MY WORRIES"
- CREATE AN ACTION PLAN - DO SOMETHING
- VISUALIZE THE END OF THE STRESS
- BREATHE

MY WORRIES

WORRY IS A SURVIVAL MECHANISM, WORRY CAN SPUR ACTION & CREATE PLANS FOR CHANGE.
EXCESSIVE WORRYING IS DRAINING & WILL IMPACT YOUR MENTAL & PHYSICAL HEALTH.
IS YOUR WORRY REALISTIC? IS IT WORTH THE WORRY?

"You can destroy your now by worrying about tomorrow."
- Janis Joplin (Singer, Songwriter)

WHAT IS WORRYING ME?
WHAT TRIGGERS YOUR WORRY?

WHY IT WORRIES ME?
LIKELIHOOD OF EVENT?
SEVERITY OF EVENT?
IS IT REALISTIC?

TAKE ACTION

~10%
REAL
WORRY?

~90%
PERCEIVED
WORRY?

WHAT CAN I DO
ABOUT IT?

DISTRACTION?
MOVEMENT?
MEDITATION?
PERSPECTIVE SHIFT?

∞
EXAMPLE

| MONEY - I DON'T HAVE ENOUGH. | IS IT A REAL WORRY? | YES? WHAT CAN I DO ABOUT IT? | EXPLORE OPTIONS | SUPPORT NETWORK | TAKING ACTION | I WILL FIND A SOLUTION! |

"Never let the future disturb you. You will meet it, if you have to, with
the same weapons of reason which today arm you against the
present." - Marcus Aurelius (Roman Emperor, Writer "Meditations")

MY SLEEP & REST

GETTING ENOUGH QUALITY SLEEP - REGULARLY, IS ONE OF THE BEST THINGS YOU CAN DO FOR YOUR BODY & MIND. IT IS NEEDED FOR A PROPERLY FUNCTIONING MACHINE - MAKE GOOD SLEEP A PRIORITY!

MY SLEEP BEST PRACTICES

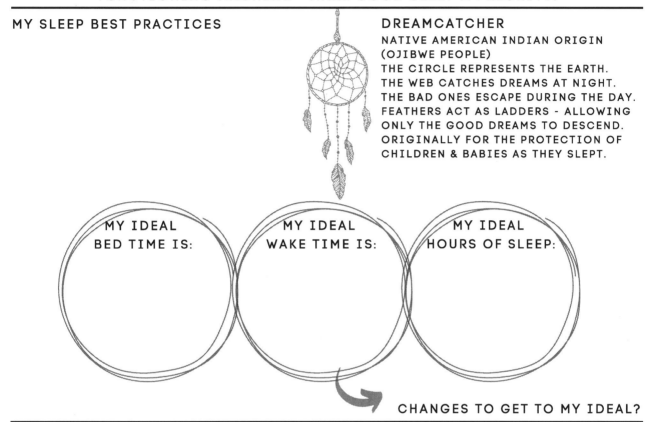

DREAMCATCHER
NATIVE AMERICAN INDIAN ORIGIN (OJIBWE PEOPLE)
THE CIRCLE REPRESENTS THE EARTH.
THE WEB CATCHES DREAMS AT NIGHT.
THE BAD ONES ESCAPE DURING THE DAY.
FEATHERS ACT AS LADDERS - ALLOWING ONLY THE GOOD DREAMS TO DESCEND.
ORIGINALLY FOR THE PROTECTION OF CHILDREN & BABIES AS THEY SLEPT.

MY IDEAL
BED TIME IS:

MY IDEAL
WAKE TIME IS:

MY IDEAL
HOURS OF SLEEP:

CHANGES TO GET TO MY IDEAL?

HOW I SWITCH OFF TO RELAX?

AIM FOR :
- DARK ROOM
- COOLER ROOM TEMPERATURE
- BED IS FOR SLEEP
- AVOID BLUE-LIGHT BEFORE BED
- REGULAR SLEEP / WAKE TIME
- BLOCK NOISE-MAKERS
- KEEP YOUR PHONE AWAY FROM BED
- MOST PEOPLE NEED 7-8 HOURS

MY TIME
TO POWER DOWN:

"We are such stuff as dreams are made on, and our little life is rounded with a sleep." - William Shakespeare (Poet)

MY STYLE

FASHION COMES FROM THE ROOT LATIN WORD "FACTIO" - "DO, MAKE". YOU CREATE YOUR OWN FASHION, YOU CAN BLEND INTO THE CROWD OR STICK-OUT FOR ALL TO ADMIRE. YOU DECIDE WHAT YOU SHOW THE WORLD - YOUR STYLE IS ALWAYS 'EN VOGUE'.

YOUR STYLE IS HOW YOU WANT THE WORLD TO SEE YOU.

WHAT PEOPLE SEE ABOUT ME

ME
AS AN ICEBERG

WHAT PEOPLE DON'T SEE ABOUT ME

MY TRENDS / STYLES/ LOOKS

THE PEOPLE AROUND YOU JUDGE YOU BASED ON "YOUR LOOK", AS YOU DO THEM. IT'S THE TIP OF THE ICEBERG YOU SHOW THE WORLD. "NOT CARING" ABOUT HOW YOU LOOK IS AS MUCH A FASHION STATEMENT AS FOLLOWING EVERY TREND. CREATE YOUR FASHION & OWN IT!

MY FASHION INSPIRATION

WHAT IMAGE DO I WANT TO PORTRAY ?

DOES IT REFLECT BELOW THE ICEBERG?

MY SUSTAINABLE FASHION

WHAT WILL I DO WITH MY DISCARDED CLOTHES?

"Real style is never right or wrong, it's a matter of being yourself: on purpose." - G. Bruce Boyer (Fashion Journalist)

"Nothing in life is to be feared, it is only to be understood. Now is the time to understand more, so that we may fear less."
- Marie Curie

WORK / CREATIVE

Your World of Work is one that can be all consuming. For some, work is life; for others, a tiresome hassle. Whatever your view on this world, it's a necessary part of a fulfilling life.

Work does not necessarily mean it's paid. While employment and one's occupation make up a big part of work, it's not the case for everyone. Homemakers, volunteers, artists, students and helpers; those who work for the aid of others, many important 'occupations' have no direct payment and some work is priceless.

While the focus on this world may seem mostly around the economic, it's only one part of this vital world. Our knowledge, learning and skill development are also essential components. Learning should be a life-long pursuit and continuing to learn new things will help you stay sharp, focused and entertained.

While you may be working for money, money itself is useless; it's what it can purchase that matters. It may seem the more you get of it, the better your life will be, but this is not always the case. While you need money to buy goods and services to survive, only up to a point will it stay motivating and increase the overall satisfaction of your life. There are many miserable millionaires. A fulfilling life is more than money.

It cannot be denied that money buys access and opens doors in the world, but it's not money at the center of fulfilling work. That belongs to your Creativity. This is when you create, make, build, or conceptualize something new, it's the collision of your learning, skills and open mindset. This can be extrinsic, something physical, like a new machine or artwork. Or it can be intrinsic, such as a new idea, joke or process.

Creativity means not accepting the status-quo. It means that you're willing to step outside the norm and look at things from other angles and perspectives. Creativity breeds confidence, resilience and intelligence. From solving problems and finding solutions, to imagination, art and design; It's something you'll try to do in this section. I know this for a fact; everyone is creative, including you, and I hope you will discover just how creative you are!

Remember, creativity is not just for artists and writers. It's about thinking outside the box, using your imagination and thinking about what's possible with whatever you are passionate about.

ALTHOUGH YOU MAY THINK YOU'RE NOT CREATIVE, THIS ISN'T CORRECT. EVERYONE HAS CREATIVITY IN SOME WAY & IN VARYING DEGREES, THE KEY IS TO FIND & UNLEASH YOURS.

WORK / CREATIVE

Passion becomes an important term in this world. Doing something you're passionate about is an important indicator you're going down the right path. You don't need to get paid for your passions, but if you want a fulfilling life, you need to incorporate your passions somehow into it. Your passions can fuel 'Flow' experiences, drive connection and increase your overall well-being.

"Flow" is the combination of your skill level and the challenge at hand, for whatever the task or activity. There are key times, when your focused energy aligns with your abilities and the challenge presents itself to give you incredible, time disrupting experiences. Learning, skill development, and allowing yourself to be challenged are key parts of fulfilling your world of work and creativity.

Your passions, like all areas on our journey also need to be kept in balance. When passion becomes your occupation, it takes on a whole new form. Back to the money! The world's economies revolve around the exchange of goods and services through the exchange of a currency, which society agrees has a certain "value". You humans have a collective trust in this currency and this allows the functioning of your large and complex societies.

Although just numbers in your bank accounts, or printed paper in your pocket, money allows you a greater freedom of choice. It also gives you a degree of power, over your own life, and potentially over others too. Power is the 'ability to influence'. A lack of money, in most societies, means less choice, health, opportunity and power. But power and money in isolation, without balance, consideration and respect, are the most corrupting influences on the planet. With power comes responsibility.

While money allows you to open doors, it also comes at a price. Your time, effort, energy, relationships, ethics and stress. It can also be a source of greed, manipulation and deceit; yet it also gives you more power over your life, and that does matter.

Although, it matters, it's also your choice the value you place on it. Is more money better, or is enough better? How much do you need? It pays to understand it. This journey may show you the personal toll of only seeking more.

Let's get into your World of Work.

WORK DEFINES INDIVIDUALS IN MANY SOCIETIES & GIVES PEOPLE A SENSE OF WORTH & IDENTITY.

**INCORPORATING YOUR CREATIVE PASSIONS INTO THIS WORLD WILL SERVE YOU WELL.
SO, LET'S START CREATING!**

PASSION
'ENTHUSIASM FOR SOMETHING; STRONG INTEREST OR DESIRE.'

WORK
'ACTIVITY INVOLVING MENTAL OR PHYSICAL EFFORT DONE IN ORDER TO ACHIEVE A PURPOSE OR RESULT.'

MOTIVATION
'THE REASON(S) ONE HAS FOR ACTING OR BEHAVING IN A PARTICULAR WAY.'

CREATIVITY
'RELATING TO OR INVOLVING THE IMAGINATION OR ORIGINAL IDEAS.'

MY CREATIVE WISDOM AT WORK

MY KNOWLEDGE BUILDING | MY NEW SKILLS TO LEARN

MY IDEAL JOB / WORK | MY CHECKLIST FOR GREAT WORK

"A truly good book teaches me better that to read it. I must soon lay it down, and commence living on its hint. what I begin reading, I must finish by acting."

- Henry David Thoreau (Natural Philosopher, Writer, Explorer)

MY FLOW

FLOW IS THE STATE OF BEING COMPLETELY IMMERSED, FULLY PRESENT & "IN THE ZONE." IT IS A BALANCE OF YOUR ABILTIES, THE CHALLENGE & YOUR FOCUS ON THE TASK. ANYONE CAN CREATE FLOW - THE MENTAL STATE IN WHICH YOUR FULFILLING WORK CAN GROW.

FLOW EXPERIENCES REQUIRE:

- INTENSE FOCUS & CONCENTRATION
- BEING FULLY ENGROSSED IN THE PRESENT MOMENT
- A SENSE OF PERSONAL CONTROL
- NATURALLY REWARDING (INTRINSICALLY)
- FEELING OF TIME IS ALTERED (FAST/SLOW)
- MERGE ACTION & AWARENESS
- DEEPLY PERSONALLY REWARDING
- WE OFTEN DON'T RECOGNIZE FLOW IN THE MOMENT, AS WE ARE TOO ENGROSSED, WE REFLECT BACK ON IT, WITH A SMILE :)

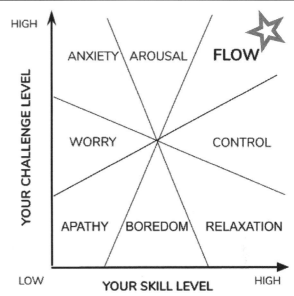

BASED ON THE WORK & RESEARCH OF HUNGARIAN-AMERICAN PSYCHOLOGIST, MIHÁLY CSÍKSZENTMIHÁLYI PH.D.

MY PAST FLOW EXPERIENCES

CREATING MORE FLOW

CURRENT SKILLS   MY NEW CHALLENGES

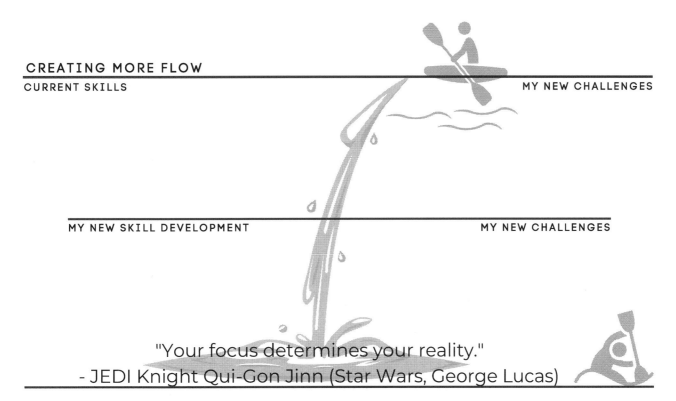

MY NEW SKILL DEVELOPMENT   MY NEW CHALLENGES

"Your focus determines your reality."
- JEDI Knight Qui-Gon Jinn (Star Wars, George Lucas)

MY PASSIONS

"PASSION" - STRONG AND BARELY CONTROLLABLE EMOTION.
ROOT WORD IS FROM LATIN "PATI" WHICH MEANS 'TO SUFFER'.

TO OVER A BILLION CHRISTIANS WORLDWIDE - PASSION - REPRESENTS THE SUFFERING OF JESUS CHRIST. YOUR PASSIONS CAN MAKE YOU SUFFER TOO, OR THEY CAN RELIEVE YOUR SUFFERING. LIVE BOTH PASSIONATELY & HARMONIOUSLY!

OBSESSIVE

- I FEEL PRESSURE FROM OUTSIDE
- I DO IT FOR THE FAME / POWER / MONEY
- I AM OVER-STIMULATED BY IT
- I OFTEN HAVE NO / LITTLE CONTROL

FEELING THE NEED TO TAKE ENDLESS PHOTOS AS TO NOT MISS A MOMENT.

HARMONIOUS

- ALIGNS WITH MY VALUES
- FEELS PART OF MY IDENTITY
- I ENJOY IT INTRINSICALLY
- I HAVE CONTROL

TAKING PHOTOS FOR THE JOY OF IT. DEVELOPING SKILL & CREATIVITY

∞ EXAMPLE

BASED ON THE DUALISTIC MODEL OF PASSION BY UNIVERSITY OF MONTREAL PROFESSOR ROBERT J. VALLERAND ET AL.

THINGS / TOPICS / STUFF THAT I LOVE DOING / BEING A PART OF.
THINGS THAT MAKE MY HEART BEAT FASTER

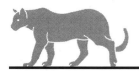

THINGS THAT I AM CURIOUS ABOUT & INTERESTED TO LEARN MORE ABOUT:
RESEARCHING & CREATING NEW PASSIONS.

"Always remember, you have within you the strength, the patience, and the passion to reach for the stars and change the world."
- Harriet Tubman (Fighter for Human Rights)

MY ACTIVE LIFE

"When you're curious, you find lots of interesting things to do."
- Walt Disney (Creator of Empires, Icons & Smiles)

INSIDE ACTIVITIES I WOULD
LIKE TO DO MORE OFTEN

OUTSIDE ACTIVITIES I WOULD
LIKE TO DO MORE OFTEN

NEW INSIDE ACTIVITIES I
WOULD LIKE TO TRY:

NEW OUTSIDE ACTIVITIES I
WOULD LIKE TO TRY:

THINGS STOPPING ME FROM
TAKING ACTION:

BENEFITS AND SOLUTIONS FROM
TAKING ACTION:

MOVING YOUR BODY TO MUSIC IS A COLLECTIVE JOY ACROSS CULTURES -
PUT ON YOUR FAVOURITE SONG & MOVE - NO SKILL OR PARTNER REQUIRED! EXAMPLE

"Dance, even if you have nowhere to do it but your own living room.
Read the directions, even if you don't follow them... "
- Baz Luhrmann (Wear Sunscreen song)

MY MENTOR - MENTEE

"MENTOR" - A TRUSTED COUNSELOR, GUIDE, COACH
"MENTEE" - PERSON RECEIVING COUNSEL FROM MENTOR

COULD I USE A MENTOR?
COULD I BE A MENTOR?

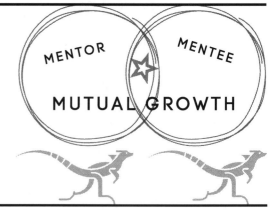

HOW CAN A MENTOR HELP ME ON MY PROFESSIONAL JOURNEY?
HOW CAN I BE A HELPFUL MENTOR TO OTHERS ON THEIRS?

WHERE COULD I FIND A MENTOR / MENTEE?   MY NETWORKING OPPORTUNITIES

A GOOD MENTOR;
- IS EXPERIENCED (THEY MAY BE WHERE YOU WANT TO BE).
- IS A GOOD LISTENER & SUPPORTS YOU IN YOUR GOALS.
- PROVIDES CONSTRUCTIVE FEEDBACK.
- HELPS YOU FIND YOUR OWN ANSWERS.
- CHALLENGES & MOTIVATES YOU.
- IS RESPECTFUL & CARES FOR YOUR WELLBEING.

MANATEE

IN THE GREEK EPIC POEM "THE ODYESSY" BY HOMER, 'MENTOR' WAS THE OLD TRUSTED FRIEND OF 'ODYSSEUS', TASKED TO EDUCATE HIS SON 'TELEMACHUS' WHILE OFF ON HIS GREAT QUEST.

"I am indebted to my father for living.
I am indebted to my teacher for living well."
- Alexander the GREAT (King, Military Leader, Empire Builder)

MY CREATIVITY

"Creativity is inventing, experimenting, growing, taking, risks, breaking rules, making mistakes, and having fun."
- Mary Lou Cook (Actress, Singer, Dancer)

MY CREATIVE SPACES

MY CREATIVE TIME

MY CREATIVE METHODS

MY CREATIVE MOODS

MY CREATIVE PROJECTS

WHAT CAN I CR∞?
"I am always doing which I cannot do, in order that I may learn how to do it." - Pablo Picasso (Painter, Creator of 'Cubism')

MY CREATIVE PROCESS

"Creativity is just connecting things." - Steve Jobs (Innovator, Creator)

UNLEASHING YOUR CREATIVITY BY UNDERSTANDING, CREATIVITY IS;

AN ABILITY

YOU HAVE THE
ABILITY
TO CREATE
SOMETHING NEW.

YOU KNEW THIS,
RIGHT?

AN ATTITUDE

ARE YOU
WILLING
TO TRY
SOMETHING
NEW?

A PROCESS

STARTS MESSY,
GETS REFINED
DEVELOPS &
BUILDS.

GIVE IT A
TRY?

IDEA GENERATION

BUILD AND DEVELOP MY IDEAS BY:
- EVOLUTION - BUILDING UPON
- SYTHESIS - COMBINING
- REVOLUTION - TWISTING VIEWS
- RE-APPLICATION - NEW USE
- CHANGE DIRECTION - NEW WAY

PMI CHART

PLUS	MINUS	INTERESTING

JOURNALISTIC SIX
WHO?
WHAT?
WHEN?
WHERE?
WHY?
HOW?

MY
IDEAS

DESIGN PROCESS
1. DEFINE / IDENTIFY
2. RESEARCH
3. IMAGINE - IDEA GENERATION
4. EVALUATE / SELECT IDEA
5. PROTOTYPE / CREATE MODEL
6. TEST / EVALUATE
7. IMPROVE

ARISTOTLE'S CATEGORIES
1. SUBSTANCE (MATERIAL)
2. QUALITY (ATTRIBUTES)
3. QUANTITY (VOLUME)
4. RELATIVES (COMPARISON)
5. PLACE (SOMEWHERE)
6. TIME (SOMETIME)
7. POSITION (LOCATION)
8. STATE (STABILITY)
9. FORCES ACTING ON (ACTIONS)
10. FORCES AFFECTING (IMPACTS)

"We need creativity in order to break-free from the temporary structures that have been set up by a particular sequence of experience."
- Dr. Edward De Bono (Physician & Author)

MY CAREER PLAN

MY CAREER GOALS

MY FIVE YEAR PLAN

MY ONE YEAR PLAN

MY SKILL DEVELOPMENT

MY SIX MONTH PLAN

"He who learns but does not think, is lost.
He who thinks but does not learn is in Great Danger." - Confucius

"If a man is called to be a street sweeper,
he should sweep streets even as
Michelangelo painted,
or Beethoven composed music
or Shakespeare composed poetry.
He should sweep streets so well that all
the hosts of Heaven and Earth will pause
to say, Here lived a GREAT street sweeper
who did his job well."

- Martin Luther King Jr.

CHRISTIAN MINISTER, CIVIL RIGHTS LEADER, NON-VIOLENT ACTIVIST.
HIS DREAM - EQUALITY FOR ALL MEN, WOMEN & CHILDREN.

MY S.W.O.T.

MY STRATEGIC PLAN FOR GROWTH,
USING MY STRENGTHS, UNDERSTANDING MY WEAKNESSES,
CAPITALIZING ON MY OPPORTUNITIES, ADAPTING TO MY THREATS

INTERNAL - I HAVE CONTROL OVER

STRENGTHS   KNOWLEDGE, SKILLS, ABILITIES, ATTRIBUTES & POSITIVE QUALITIES

EG. I AM STRONG & RESILIENT

WEAKNESSES   WHATS HOLDING ME BACK? STUMBLING BLOCKS - THINGS TO LEARN

EG. I TEND TO EAT CLOSE TO BIG SHARKS

EXTERNAL - I HAVE NO / LITTLE CONTROL OVER

OPPORTUNITIES   MY MANY POSSIBILITIES TO EXPLORE

EG. A VAST OCEAN TO EXPLORE

THREATS   MY CHALLENGES I HAVE TO ACKNOWLEDGE / OVERCOME / HANDLE

EG. CLIMATE CHANGE

MY LEARNING

"Education is the kindling of a flame, not the filling of a vessel."
- Socrates (Ancient Greek Teacher of Plato, who taught Aristotle...)

MY LEARNING STYLE - V.A.R.K. MODEL
WHAT ARE YOUR LEARNING STYLES? YOU MAY FAVOUR ONE, BUT ALL CAN BE EFFECTIVE

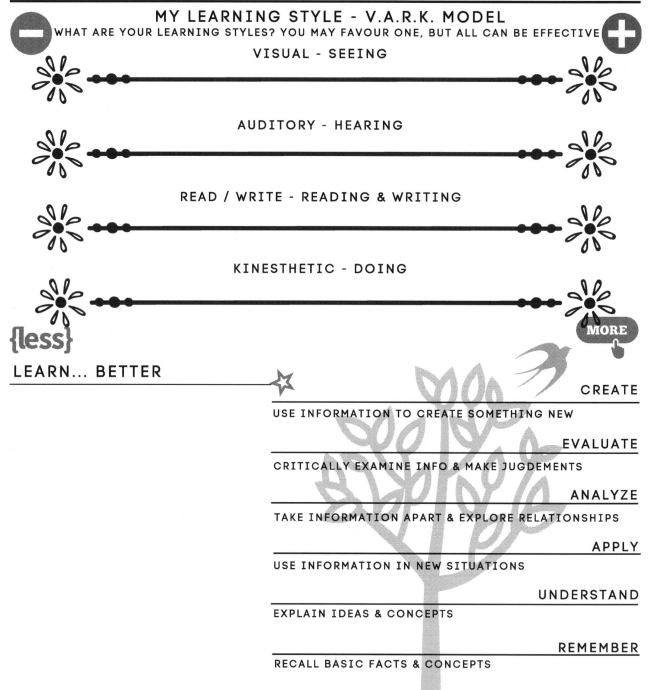

VISUAL - SEEING

AUDITORY - HEARING

READ / WRITE - READING & WRITING

KINESTHETIC - DOING

{less}

MORE

LEARN... BETTER

CREATE
USE INFORMATION TO CREATE SOMETHING NEW

EVALUATE
CRITICALLY EXAMINE INFO & MAKE JUGDEMENTS

ANALYZE
TAKE INFORMATION APART & EXPLORE RELATIONSHIPS

APPLY
USE INFORMATION IN NEW SITUATIONS

UNDERSTAND
EXPLAIN IDEAS & CONCEPTS

REMEMBER
RECALL BASIC FACTS & CONCEPTS

EACH HAS THEIR TIME & NEED - WITH AN AIM TO BUILD TO HIGHER LEARNING -
WHERE IS YOUR LEARNING HAPPENING? - BASED ON BLOOM'S TAXONOMY

"What any person in the world can learn, almost all persons can learn if provided with appropriate prior and current conditions of learning."
- Benjamin Bloom (Educational Psychologist & Researcher)

MY MONEY

"Too many people spend money they haven't earned, to buy things they don't want, to impress people they don't like."
- Will Rogers (Actor, Columnist, World Explorer)

HOW CAN I EARN MORE?
(HOW MUCH DO I NEED?)

HOW CAN I SAVE MORE?

PROMOTION, DEVELOP SKILLS, NETWORKING, INVESTING, SIDE-BUSINESS, SALES?

HOW CAN I PUT MONEY AWAY FOR THE UNEXPECTED OR FUTURE NEEDS?

NEW INCOME SOURCES?
(THAT ALIGN WITH MY VALUES)

HOW CAN I CUT DOWN COSTS / REDUCE DEBT?

NEW BUSINESS? NEW INVESTMENTS? NEW CAREER? NEW SKILLS? CREATING NEW?

AM I SPENDING MORE THAN I EARN? AM I HAPPY WITH MY DEBT LEVEL?

MY FINANCES

UNDERSTAND YOUR FINANCES. THE BASICS YOU NEED TO THINK ABOUT.

MY SOURCES OF INCOME
MONTHLY

FIXED EXPENSES
DON'T CHANGE / MONTH

COSTS I **NEED** TO COVER

VARIABLE EXPENSES
CHANGE MONTHLY

ONCE THIS IS COVERED
THIS IS LEFTOVER

WHAT I **WANT** TO SPEND ON
PRIORITIZE

THINK ABOUT HAVING AN EMERGENCY FUND, DEVELOPING MULTIPLE SOURCES OF INCOME & CREATING A BUDGET TO KEEP ON TRACK. GET TRUSTED FINANCIAL ADVICE!

MY SAVINGS

MY INVESTMENTS

MY DEBTS

"The price of anything is the amount of life you exchange for it."
- Henry David Thoreau

MY INVESTMENTS

INVEST - COMES FROM "TO CLOTHE"
YOU WANT TO CLOTHE YOURSELF FOR YOUR BEST FUTURE.

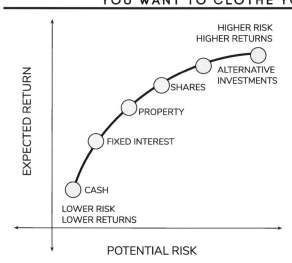

THIS IS A MODEL TO UNDERSTAND HOW 'RETURN ON INVESTMENT' (R.O.I.) RELATES TO RISK. CASH DOESN'T ACCURE INTEREST, SO NO RETURN. IT'S LOW RISK AS YOU HAVE IT IN YOUR HAND, ONE COULD EQUALLY ARGUE, KEEPING TOO MUCH CASH IS HIGH RISK; AS WOULD BE INVESTING IN A MARKETING SCHEME 'GUARANTEEING' HIGH RETURNS. DON'T LET SOMEONE TAKE THE CLOTHES OFF YOUR BACK! UNDERSTAND YOUR INVESTMENTS & RISK TOLERANCE.

MY FUTURE
WHAT AM I DOING TO INVEST IN MY FUTURE?

MY MONEY / RESOURCES
IS MY MONEY WORKING FOR ME?

LIKE WITH MANY THINGS
IN LIFE; IT'S A BALANCE

MY TIME / ENERGY
AM I GETTING TRUSTED FINANCIAL ADVICE?

1. "NEVER DEPEND ON A SINGLE INCOME. MAKE INVESTMENTS TO CREATE A SECOND SOURCE."
2. "IF YOU BUY THINGS YOU DON'T NEED, SOON YOU WILL HAVE TO SELL THINGS YOU NEED."
3. "DO NOT SAVE WHAT IS LEFT AFTER SPENDING, BUT SPEND WHAT IS LEFT AFTER SAVING"
4. "NEVER TEST THE DEPTH OF THE RIVER WITH TWO FEET."
5. "DO NOT PUT ALL YOUR EGGS IN ONE BASKET."
- WARREN BUFFET (BILLIONAIRE INVESTOR & PHILANTHROPIST)

MY RISK

"You have to take risks. We will only understand the miracle of life fully when we allow the unexpected to happen."
- Paulo Coelho (Writer - 'The Alchemist')

WHAT'S MY REACTION TO RISK?

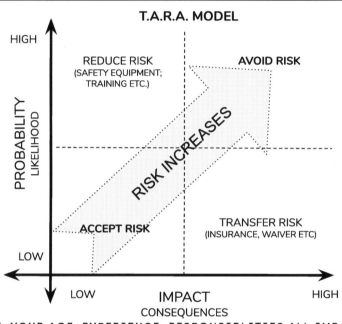

T.A.R.A. MODEL

HIGH

PROBABILITY LIKELIHOOD

REDUCE RISK (SAFETY EQUIPMENT; TRAINING ETC.)

AVOID RISK

RISK INCREASES

ACCEPT RISK

TRANSFER RISK (INSURANCE, WAIVER ETC)

LOW

LOW   IMPACT   HIGH
          CONSEQUENCES

RISK IS A PART OF LIFE, YOUR AGE, EXPERIENCE, RESPONSIBLITIES ALL IMPACT YOUR RISK ASSESSMENT. UNDERSTAND YOUR RISK / REWARD BALANCE.

I NEED TO FIND MY OWN "SWEET SPOT" DEPENDING ON THE SITUATION

AM I ACCURATELY WEIGHING UP MY RISKS?

<u>LIFETIME RISK OF DEATH (USA):</u>
1 : 5 - HEART DISEASE
1 : 7 - CANCER
1 : 63 - INFLUENZA
1 : 84 - CAR ACCIDENT
1 : 4919 - BIKE ACCIDENT
1 : 5,051 - AIR ACCIDENT
1 : 79,746 - HIT BY LIGHTENING
1 : 3,748,067 - SHARK ATTACK

SOURCE - FLORIDA MUSEUM (USA)

WHICH IS MORE RISKY?
A GREAT WHITE SHARK, OR THE MODERN, GREAT APE DIET?

MANAGING YOUR RISK, UNDERSTANDING RISK. IT'S PERSONAL. AS THE STATISTICS SHOW MAYBE YOUR LIFE'S BIGGEST RISK FACTOR IS IN THE CHOICES YOU MAKE, EVERYDAY...

"Twenty years from now you will be more disappointed by the things that you didn't do than by the ones you did do."
- Mark Twain (Writer, Humorist, Entrepreneur, Publisher)

MY SMALL GOALS

"Little by little, one walks far." - Peruvian Proverb

GOAL = "THE END TOWARD WHICH EFFORT IS DIRECTED"

WHAT ARE YOUR DESIRED OUTCOMES? - SEE HOW YOUR SPECIFIC GOALS CAN GET YOU THE OUTCOMES YOUR DESIRE? BUT WHAT ARE THE OUTCOMES YOU DESIRE?

SMART GOALS - FOR SHORTER TERM ACCOMPLISHMENT

S
SPECIFIC

M
MEASUREABLE

A
ACHIEVEABLE

R
RELEVANT

T
TIME-BOUND

LOSE 5KG IN 8 WEEKS TO BE READY FOR MY BEST FRIEND'S WEDDING ∞ EXAMPLE

SMALL GOALS - FOR SUSTAINABLE & LIFE LONG ACHIEVEMENT

S
SPECIFIC

M
MEASUREABLE

A
ACTION - ORIENTED

L
LIFE - LINKED

L
LONG-TERM

WORKOUT 5 DAYS A WEEK CONSISTENLY TO IMPROVE MY STRENGTH, HEALTH & CONFIDENCE, WHICH WILL MAKE ME FEEL EMPOWERED. ∞ EXAMPLE

"The greater danger for most of us isn't that our aim is too high and miss it, but that it is too low and we reach it."

- Michelangelo (Renaissance Painter/Sculptor - Sistine Chapel Ceiling)

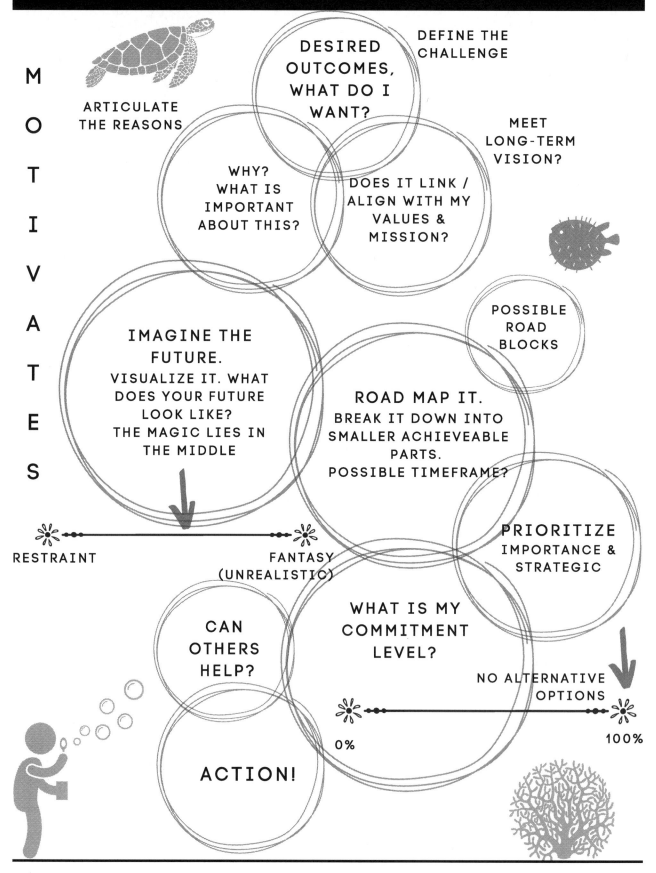

MOTIVATES

ARTICULATE THE REASONS

DESIRED OUTCOMES, WHAT DO I WANT?

DEFINE THE CHALLENGE

MEET LONG-TERM VISION?

WHY? WHAT IS IMPORTANT ABOUT THIS?

DOES IT LINK / ALIGN WITH MY VALUES & MISSION?

POSSIBLE ROAD BLOCKS

IMAGINE THE FUTURE. VISUALIZE IT. WHAT DOES YOUR FUTURE LOOK LIKE? THE MAGIC LIES IN THE MIDDLE

ROAD MAP IT. BREAK IT DOWN INTO SMALLER ACHIEVEABLE PARTS. POSSIBLE TIMEFRAME?

PRIORITIZE IMPORTANCE & STRATEGIC

RESTRAINT

FANTASY (UNREALISTIC)

CAN OTHERS HELP?

WHAT IS MY COMMITMENT LEVEL?

NO ALTERNATIVE OPTIONS

ACTION!

0%

100%

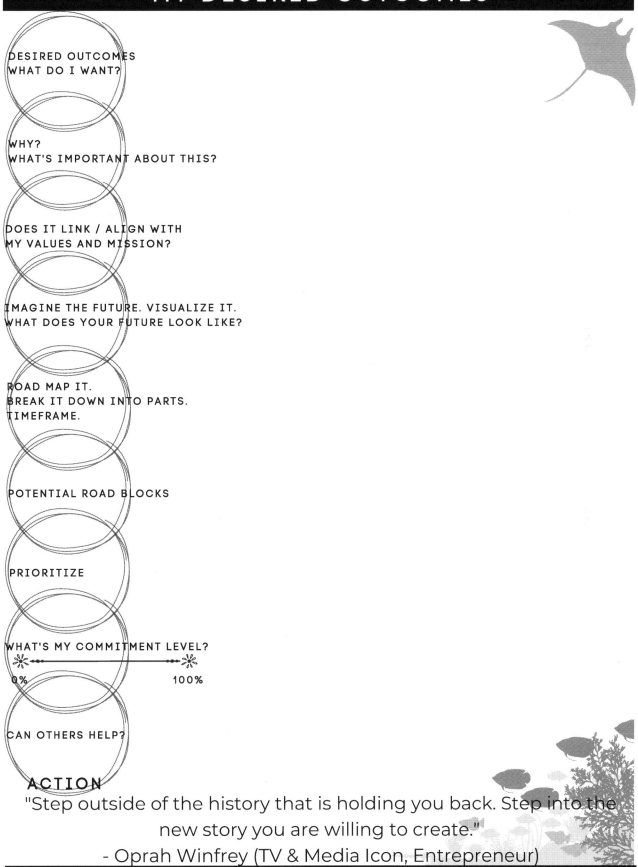

DESIRED OUTCOMES
WHAT DO I WANT?

WHY?
WHAT'S IMPORTANT ABOUT THIS?

DOES IT LINK / ALIGN WITH
MY VALUES AND MISSION?

IMAGINE THE FUTURE. VISUALIZE IT.
WHAT DOES YOUR FUTURE LOOK LIKE?

ROAD MAP IT.
BREAK IT DOWN INTO PARTS.
TIMEFRAME.

POTENTIAL ROAD BLOCKS

PRIORITIZE

WHAT'S MY COMMITMENT LEVEL?

0%   100%

CAN OTHERS HELP?

ACTION

"Step outside of the history that is holding you back. Step into the
new story you are willing to create."
- Oprah Winfrey (TV & Media Icon, Entrepreneur)

TECHNOLOGICAL
MY GOALS / OUTCOMES

"May your choices reflect your hopes, not your fears."
- Nelson Mandela

TECHNOLOGICAL

Your most recent World is that of the Technological. Although technological innovations have occurred throughout human history, few have had the swift, dramatic and universal upheaval of the last 20 to 30 years or so.

The internet, smartphones, interactive video games, streaming, social media, apps, I.o.T., A.i., the list grows by the day. The world is now tightly interconnected through a digital framework that no one controls or governs. Is the world controlled by people and their devices? Or are the devices controlling the people?

Technology provides you with endless entertainment, convenience and communication options. You can now interact directly with your favourite celebrities, or facetime with your family from anywhere in the world. The change has been quick and dramatic. In just over a decade the way you communicate, co-operate and cohabitate have all changed. The human brain and emotional systems have had to adapt very quickly and it hasn't always been an easy ride.

Access to endless news and information is a double-edged sword. We're now better informed than ever before, but the 24/7 news-cycle and hunt for clicks means it's harder to spot the real from the fake. Endless notifications keep us alert and in a state of higher panic. The world seems more dangerous than ever before, even though, on many metrics, the world has never been safer.

For many, the information they receive has only reinforced their biases. Can you trust what you see on your newsfeed?

You want tech to work for you, not be controlled by it. Well, I am assuming that fact. Technology companies have deliberately made their devices and software leaving you wanting more. They will try to hook you, with the aim to take as much of your attention as possible. They monetize your attention. Nothing is free, your time and your attention have value. You are now tracked, traced and watched; leaving a digital footprint wherever you go. While you scroll, they watch and get paid, don't forget that.

Social media has the potential to connect people in helpful new ways, but it has also become a 'grossly exaggerated reality'; or in my book club, we call it "a fake reality". Carefully crafted, you watch the lives of others, but you compare your 'real-life' to their 'fake-reality'. One of the worst things you humans can do is blindly compare your lives to that of others and today, instead of comparing yourself to your real neighbours, you judge your life based on the air-brushed lives of celebrities and few billion others, no wonder the self-esteem issues humans are having! Personally, I would suggest better use of your time, but that is my book bias kicking in.

Where you put your attention is your decision. You can choose to focus on your real life or your digital life? Your can choose to compare your real life to the digital lives of others? Whatever the life, we're all seeing it through different filters, be that Instagram or otherwise. As a book, I just think you should you be creating your own adventures and writing your own amazing story.

YOUR ATTENTION IS VALUABLE & MANY COMPANIES ARE TRYING TO TAKE YOURS. WHERE IS YOUR ATTENTION FOCUSED?

'ATTENTION'

FROM "ATTEND" "BE PRESENT AT"

ATTENTION =
YOU HAVE THE CHOICE WHERE TO PUT YOURS!

TECHNOLOGICAL

Your relationship with technology, like with anything, should be in balance with the rest of your life. For many people, their digital world has become their real world.

Your real world is where your brains and bodies and relationships actually live, but these can be sidelined and sacrificed for the ease, anonymity and pleasure-seeking of the digital-life. For better or for worse, technology is now helping you make decisions, providing you with emotional support and shaping your identity.

Getting the most out of your tech means making the most of the practical, useful, convenient stuff; and limiting the time-wasting, soul-degrading, self-esteem crashing stuff. Knowing the difference is half the battle. Knowledge is power, because the more you know, the more you can see the tactics engineers and marketers use to pull you in and sap away your precious attention.

The blur between the real and the digital is now life. You live both online and offline lives, in various ways and extremes, but chances are, if you have this in your hand, you have a screen very close by. How you choose to post, comment, share, like and emoji bomb is completely up to you. But realize too, that these have consequences that can be impossible to erase. It's good to have your own guidelines for online interaction that align with the person you are, offline.

Losing yourself in the digital world is a rabbit hole; that nobody knows what the true long-term consequences are. After all, it hasn't been around long enough to really know. Some research has shown if you are going to use social media, be engaged in it rather than just watch from the sidelines. If you aren't engaged (positively) it's probably best to find better use of your time.

Are you your 'true-self' when we are online? Are you being authentic? The key to bring tech into your life, and get the most out of it, is to understand it. Know how you react to it and understand how it controls you; then you can take back control and choose to interact.

Your technological use is linked to your physical health and mental health, your social connections and intimate lives. Living your best life is about getting the best out of technology without letting it take control. Do you have control over your tech? Or is your tech controlling you and your well-being?

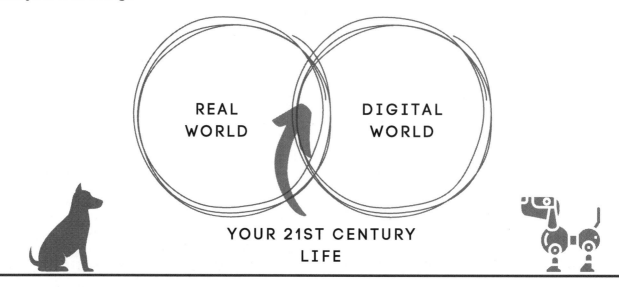

REAL WORLD   DIGITAL WORLD

YOUR 21ST CENTURY LIFE

TECHNOLOGICAL
MY DIGITAL WORLD

THE TECH I CAN'T LIVE WITHOUT!

BALANCING MY SCREENTIME

1
0
1
0
1
0
1
0
1
0
1
0
1
0
1
0
1
0
1
0
1
0
1
0
1
0
1
0
1
0
1
0
1
0
1
0

MY NEW TECH 'LIFE-HACKS'

WHAT CAN I OUTSOURCE?

∞
EXAMPLE

"HACK" - 'CUT' OR 'SEVER' - A "LIFE HACK" IS
A SHORT-CUT OR EASIER / QUICKER
WAY TO DO SOMETHING; HERE - USING TECH
TO HELP FREE UP YOUR TIME

CAN I GET SOMEONE ELSE TO DO THINGS THAT
MAKE SENSE - BASED ON MY LIMITED TIME /
SKILLS / NEEDS?
EG TAXES, MARKETING, LOGISTICS

"Imagination is more important than knowledge. For knowledge is
limited to all we know and understand, while imagination embraces
the entire world, and all there ever will be to know and understand."
- Albert Einstein (Dreamer, Discoverer, Pioneer)

MY TECH USES

"The internet is becoming the town square for the global village of tomorrow." - Bill Gates (Founder of 'Microsoft', Philanthropist)

FUNCTIONAL - MY USEFUL USES

∞
EXAMPLE
COMMUNICATION TOOLS, MAPS, SEARCH

CREATIONAL - MY CREATIVE USES

VIDEO / PHOTO / AUDIO CREATION

RECREATIONAL - MY FUN USES

GAMES, QUIZZES, MUSIC

BY RECOGNIZING & APPRECIATING THE DIFFERENT USES OF TECH, YOU ARE UNDERSTANDING HOW & WHERE TO BEST USE IT.

"Technology is a useful servant but a dangerous master."
- Christian Lous Lange (Norwegian Historian, Scientist)

MY (SMART)PHONE

DO I CONTROL MY PHONE?

AM I HAPPY WITH HOW / HOW MUCH I USE MY PHONE?

HAS MY PHONE USAGE CAUSED PROBLEMS OR ISSUES WITH OTHERS?

IF SO, HOW?

WHAT DO I USE MY PHONE MOST FOR?

COMMUNICATION, FUN, FUNCTIONAL, CREATIVE?

CAN I BETTER MANAGE MY PHONE USE?

MANAGE MY PHONE

- BE AWARE OF YOUR USAGE
- TURN OFF / PAUSE NOTIFICATIONS
- PROTECT YOUR SLEEP
- BE PRESENT
- UNDERSTAND THE DISTRACTION
- AIRPLANE MODE FOR PEACE
- MAKE TIME TO RE-CHARGE WITHOUT

CREATE PHONE-FREE TIME
BE PRESENT IN THE REAL WORLD WITHOUT DISTRACTIONS

MY PHONE BEST PRACTICES

"The challenges for a human now is to be more interesting to another than his or her smartphone." - Alain de Botton (Author, Philosopher)

"Don't keep forever on the public road, going only where others have gone, and following one after the other like a flock of sheep.
Leave the beaten track occasionally and dive into the woods.
Every time you do so you will be certain to find something that you have never seen before."

- Alexander Graham Bell

MY MOBILE BEST PRACTICES

"BEST PRACTICES" - YOUR OWN GUIDELINES OR IDEAS THAT REPRESENT YOUR MOST EFFECTIVE COURSE OF ACTION; WHERE YOU OBTAIN OPTIMAL RESULTS. LIVING THE MOMENTS THAT MATTER, IN REAL LIFE.

IN THE EVENING / BEFORE BED

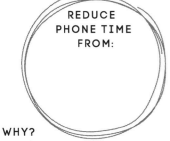

REDUCE PHONE TIME FROM:

WHY?
BLUELIGHT / STIMULATION CAN DISRUPT SLEEP & MAKE IT HARD TO FALL ASLEEP.

WHILE AT WORK/SCHOOL/DAY

WHY?
IT DISTRACTS YOUR FOCUS - GOOD FOR BREAKS - NOT FOR CONCENTRATION.

WHILE INTERACTING WITH OTHERS IN-PERSON

WHY?
YOU'RE DISTRACTED, YOU AREN'T REALLY LISTENING OR FOCUSED TO THE PERSON YOU ARE WITH.

WHILE WITH THE ONES I LOVE

WHY?
THE QUICKEST WAY TO BREAK PERSONAL INTIMACY & REAL CONNECTION.

REMEMBER! YOUR MOBILE OFFERS MANY CONVENIENCES, BUT IT'S ALSO A BIG DISTRACTION - IT CAN TAKE AWAY YOUR FOCUS & CONCENTRATION. IF YOU DON'T HAVE POWER OVER YOUR PHONE, IT WILL EXERT POWER OVER YOU! MAKE YOUR TECHNOLOGY WORK FOR YOU!

MY TECH-FELT EMOTIONS

HOW DOES YOUR TECHNOLOGY USE MAKE YOU FEEL AFTER USING IT? THINK ABOUT IT? & BE HONEST WITH YOURSELF.

HOW DO I FEEL AFTER LONG-BOUTS OF TECH USE?
BINGE WATCHING OR MARATHON GAMING?

I FEEL TERRIBLE!   I FEEL AMAZING!

HOW DO I FEEL AFTER USING SOCIAL MEDIA?

I FEEL TERRIBLE!   I FEEL AMAZING!

HOW DO I FEEL AFTER READING / SCROLLING NEWS?

I FEEL TERRIBLE!   I FEEL AMAZING!

HOW DO I FEEL WHEN I CREATE SOMETHING ORIGINAL?

I FEEL TERRIBLE!   I FEEL AMAZING!

HOW DO I FEEL WHEN I AM ALONE (WITHOUT MY TECH)?

I FEEL TERRIBLE!   I FEEL AMAZING!

HOW DO I FEEL WHEN I AM LEARNING SOMETHING I WANT TO LEARN?

I FEEL TERRIBLE!   I FEEL AMAZING!

"If we teach today as we taught yesterday, we rob our children of tomorrow." - John Dewey (Educator)

MY SOCIAL MEDIA #BESTPRACTICES

SOCIAL MEDIA HAS HUGE POWER TO BRING PEOPLE TOGETHER; EQUALLY, IT
HAS THE POTENTIAL TO SPREAD LIES & MIS-TRUTHS,
AND; IF NOT CAREFUL, SLOWLY TAKE COMMAND OF YOUR LIFE.

MY POSTING

MY COMMENTING

1
0
1
0
1
0
1
0
1
0
1
0
1
0
1
0
1
0
1
0
1
0
1
0
1
0
1
0
1
0
1
0
1
0
1
0
1
0
1
0
1

MY CRITICS

MY RELIABLE SOURCES OF
INFORMATION

TRUTH
REALITY

FICTION
FAKE

SOCIAL MEDIA =
#FAKEREALITY
ENSURE YOU
UNDERSTAND
WHAT SOCIAL MEDIA
IS FOR A
#BETTERYOU

"Your time is limited, so don't waste it on living someone else's life."
- Steve Jobs (Creator of the Smartphone)

MY TECHNO- INTIMATE WORLD

"Technology appeals to us most where we are most vulnerable."
- Sherry Turkle (Researcher, Author - "Alone Together")

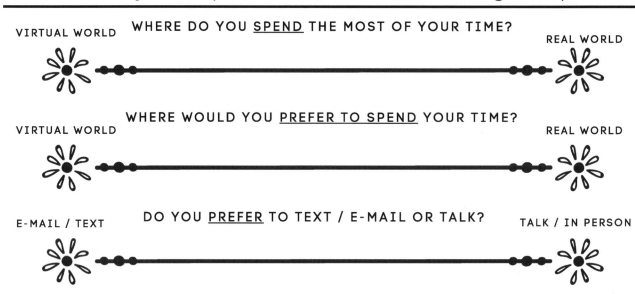

WHERE DO YOU <u>SPEND</u> THE MOST OF YOUR TIME?

VIRTUAL WORLD   REAL WORLD

WHERE WOULD YOU <u>PREFER TO SPEND</u> YOUR TIME?

VIRTUAL WORLD   REAL WORLD

DO YOU <u>PREFER</u> TO TEXT / E-MAIL OR TALK?

E-MAIL / TEXT   TALK / IN PERSON

<u>TO THE RESPONSE TO EACH OF YOUR QUESTIONS. WHY?</u>

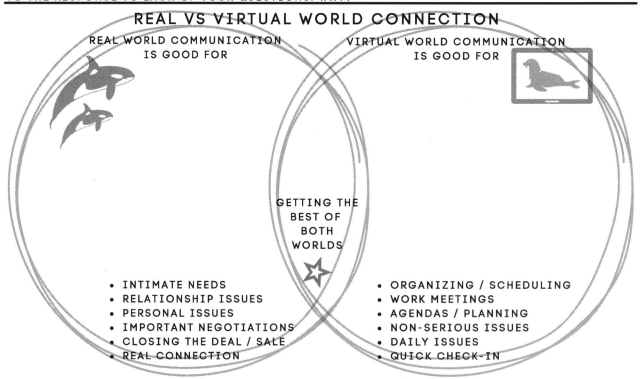

REAL VS VIRTUAL WORLD CONNECTION

REAL WORLD COMMUNICATION
IS GOOD FOR

VIRTUAL WORLD COMMUNICATION
IS GOOD FOR

GETTING THE
BEST OF
BOTH
WORLDS

- INTIMATE NEEDS
- RELATIONSHIP ISSUES
- PERSONAL ISSUES
- IMPORTANT NEGOTIATIONS
- CLOSING THE DEAL / SALE
- REAL CONNECTION

- ORGANIZING / SCHEDULING
- WORK MEETINGS
- AGENDAS / PLANNING
- NON-SERIOUS ISSUES
- DAILY ISSUES
- QUICK CHECK-IN

EVER TRIED TO SOLVE A SERIOUS RELATIONSHIP ISSUE OVER TEXT?
MOST LIKELY OUTCOME - FAIL. KNOW WHEN TO USE TECH & WHEN TO AVOID IT.
CHOOSE THE BEST MEDIUM OF COMMUNCATION FOR THE NEED AT HAND. ∞ EXAMPLE

"Being alone feels like a problem that needs to be solved."
- Sherry Turkle (Researcher, Teacher)   (EXPLORE "ME, MYSELF & I" PG 141)

MY APPS
MY TOP 10 APPS

	APP NAME	CURRENT USAGE	DESIRED USAGE
1			
2			
3			
4			
5			
6			
7			
8			
9			
10			

KNOW WHERE YOU SPEND YOU DIGITAL ATTENTION - IS IT OPTIMAL?
1. TOO MUCH; 2. ABOUT RIGHT; 3.NOT ENOUGH

MY TECH TIME

THE MORE YOU UNDERSTAND WHERE YOU SPEND YOUR TIME, THE MORE TIME YOU WILL HAVE. KNOW WHERE YOU SPEND YOURS.

MY TECH	MY DAILY TIME	MY WEEKLY TIME	MY OPTIMAL TIME	CHANGE?
STREAMING NETFLIX YOUTUBE PRIME \ DISNEY INCLUDES BINGE WATCHING				
T.V. LIVE, ONDEMAND, PVR				
BROWSING THE WWW SURFING, ONLINE SHOPPING				
SOCIAL MEDIA FACEBOOK, TWITTER, INSTAGRAM, TIKTOK...				
VIDEO GAMES XBOX, PLAYSTATION, ONLINE.				
NEWS MEDIA NEWS APPS, WEBSITES, BLOGS.				
GIZMOS GADGETS, WATCHES, ETC ETC.				

"Time is the most valuable thing a man can spend."

-Theophrastus (Greek Philosopher, Botanist, Scientist, Teacher)

MY INFORMATION

"A reliable way to make people believe in falsehoods is frequent repetition, because familiarity is not easily distinguished from truth. Authoritarian institutions and marketers have always known this fact."
- Daniel Kahneman (Author, Psychologist, Economist)

WHERE DO I GET MOST OF MY NEWS / INFORMATION?

KEEPING MYSELF UP TO DATE ABOUT THE WORLD I LIVE

HOW CAN I ENSURE I CAN TRUST MY SOURCES OF INFORMATION?

I WANT THE TRUTH; OR AS CLOSE TO THE TRUTH AS POSSIBLE!

HOW CAN I DIVERSIFY MY INFORMATION SOURCES?

THERE ARE MANY PERSPECTIVES. I WANT TO MAKE MY OWN OPINION, NOT BE TOLD IT

HOW CAN I BETTER SPOT FAKE STORIES ONLINE?

FAKE NEWS CHECKLIST:
- CONSIDER THE SOURCE
- WHAT'S THEIR MOTIVATION?
- CHECK THE AUTHOR
- READ BEYOND THE HEADLINE
- IS IT SUPPORTED?
- CHECK THE DATE
- CHECK YOUR BIASES
- IS IT A JOKE?
- ASK FOR HELP

"The more often a stupidity is reported, the more it gets the appearance of wisdom." - Voltaire (French Philosopher)

THE ENDLESS KNOT

THE ENDLESS KNOT SYMBOLIZES LIFE AS AN ENDLESS CYCLE;
OF A UNION & HARMONY WITH THE UNIVERSE; OF WHOLENESS.
IT MAY SEEM AS THERE ARE SEPERATE PARTS,
BUT JUST LIKE A CIRCLE - IT'S JUST ONE COMPLETE UNBROKEN LINE
NO BEGINNING, NO END & NO SEPERATION.

"Humankind has not woven the web of life.
We are but one thread within it.
Whatever we do to the web, we do to
ourselves.
All things are bound together.
All things connect."

- Chief Seattle

THE ENDLESS KNOT DATES BACK TO AT LEAST 2500BC - FOUND FIRST IN THE INDUS VALLEY
(PAKISTAN) - THESE SYMBOLS HAVE BEEN PASSED ON BY HUMANS FOR MILLENNIA. IT HAS
IMPORTANT SYMBOLISM ACROSS CULTURES; IN BUDDHISM, JAINISM, CHINESE PHILOSOPHY; AS
WELL AS FOR CELTIC PAGANS & CHRISTIANS IN EUROPE & BEYOND.
ALL IS BOUND IN AN ENDLESS KNOT.

INTIMATE
MY GOALS / OUTCOMES

"It matters not who you love, where you love,
why you love, when you love or how you love,
it matters only that you love."
- John Lennon

INTIMATE

Intimacy is personal, social and emotional. Unlike a purely social interaction, your Intimate World requires a deeper look at your most personal desires, needs and emotions. At the center of intimacy is Trust, be that with yourself or someone else.

Intimacy means to be genuinely open and honest, a feeling of connection, of closeness and support. Usually this is with another person, but you can also have intimate moments alone, and in nature, or when you feel a deep connection with other life.

This world is the home of your emotions. Emotions are those feelings that make you happy, sad, scared and lonely. There are many triggers to your emotions, some seem rational responses to stimuli, others seem irrational and uncontrollable. Your emotions determine how you feel, but they also impact your thoughts and decisions.

Your heart is considered the center of your emotional world. When you feel something, you feel it inside you, in your heart and gut, more than in your head. In fact, both your heart and gut have their own brain and nervous systems. The heart's 'Intrinsic Cardiac Nervous System' and the 'Enteric Nervous System' of the gut. They are completely separate brains, with brain cells, in your chest. Your heart/gut - head conflict feels very real and maybe it is your major energy centers in debate?

Along with the heart comes the emotion most associated with it, love. Love is an emotion and arguably our strongest of all. Love has been the most influential theme in music, movies and literature. Humans have been known to do more for love than any other emotion. You may have heard the phrase, "Love is a drug", and actually, it's quite true. Love, like your other emotions, are chemical reactions inside you. They are reactions to stimuli and the way your body/mind makes sense of the world around it.

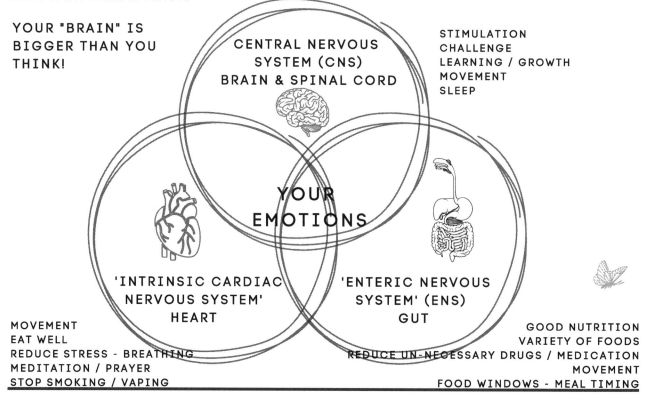

YOUR "BRAIN" IS
BIGGER THAN YOU
THINK!

CENTRAL NERVOUS
SYSTEM (CNS)
BRAIN & SPINAL CORD

STIMULATION
CHALLENGE
LEARNING / GROWTH
MOVEMENT
SLEEP

YOUR
EMOTIONS

'INTRINSIC CARDIAC
NERVOUS SYSTEM'
HEART

'ENTERIC NERVOUS
SYSTEM' (ENS)
GUT

MOVEMENT
EAT WELL
REDUCE STRESS - BREATHING
MEDITATION / PRAYER
STOP SMOKING / VAPING

GOOD NUTRITION
VARIETY OF FOODS
REDUCE UN-NECESSARY DRUGS / MEDICATION
MOVEMENT
FOOD WINDOWS - MEAL TIMING

INTIMATE

Love is not your only emotion of course. Along with the good, there is also the opposite; disgust, anger. Your emotions have their use, you would not want to feel love with a lion running after you, fear will motivate you to find safety... hopefully.

Thankfully, your emotions are also temporary. While it may not always feel like it, your emotions are in constant flux. The chemicals produced and released in the various organs and glands cause feelings in your body to change, both with time and stimulus. Adaptation is one of humanity's greatest assets, but the downside is that both your body and mind adapt to the new, so the new becomes old, and less exciting. Remember how nervous you were on your first day of work / school? Or the first kiss with your "Significant Other"?

Sometimes you make permanent decisions based on these fleeting emotions and then have to live with the consequences. This is often called an 'emotional decision' and emotional decision-making is typically seen as less reliable over the longer term.

Developing more direct influence and control over your emotions is called 'Emotional Intelligence'. Instead of your emotions controlling you, you take more control over your emotions. It's not about suppression or denial, it's about reacting the way you want to react in a situation and not being a victim of your emotional response (and those chemicals racing around your body).

> 'EMOTIONAL INTELLIGENCE'
>
> 'THE CAPACITY TO BE AWARE OF; CONTROL & EXPRESS ONES EMOTIONS; RESPOND APPROPRIATELY TO THE EMOTIONS OF OTHERS.'

It starts with awareness, before you can truly become more emotionally in-control, you first need to look at yourself. You are your most intimate cheerleader and critic. By better understanding your intimate world, you open yourself up to more fulfilling and trusting relationships, including trusting in yourself, you know this as;
Self-Confidence.

How do you express intimacy? If you're willing to, you can open up your vulnerable side in this section, and you may be pleasantly surprised. I know, just going through this process will be valuable to you. It's about trust and the feeling you can be authentic, both with yourself and with others.

Many equate intimacy with the physical actions around sex. This can be part of intimacy, but only one part. Sex does not need to play any role in a fulfilling intimate experience or relationship, but that will depend on you. Physical touch and closeness are beneficial for all humans. This can be as simple as a held-hand or loving hug. There are different steps of intimacy and different comfort zones you have in different situations. Your comfort zone is for you to set and explore. Respect and trust is at the core of all healthy intimate relationships.

Pushing out of your comfort zone in positive ways will cause growth in all your worlds. There is no way to grow a muscle without stress, just as there is no way to know your potential without getting "butterflies". You know? That feeling in your gut!
As the saying goes, "Your comfort zone is a beautiful place, but nothing grows there." This means tackling the unknown, it can also mean facing your fears. Butterflies should signal to you that you are on a brave new adventure. Remember, your aim is to simply make your butterflies fly in formation. You DO NOT want to kill your butterflies. You want to cultivate them and get to know them. Now fly butterflies, fly!

INTIMATE
MY LOVE & EMOTIONS

CREATE INTIMATE TIME

WHAT I VALUE IN A PARTNERSHIP?

HOW I BUILD TRUST:

TRUST
THE CENTER OF
INTIMACY

BECOMING A BETTER
COMMUNICATOR:

CREATE MORE INTIMACY BY:
- ALLOWING YOURSELF TO BE AUTHENTIC
- TRUSTING YOURSELF
- LISTENING ACTIVELY
- SHOWING YOU CARE
- SHARING YOUR REAL STORY (WITH THOSE YOU TRUST)
- CREATING SOMETHING WITH ANOTHER
- HUGGING - DANCING - TOUCH (WHERE APPROPRIATE)
- SHARING AN ADVENTURE
- SHARING LAUGHTER
- OFFERING YOUR GENUINE HELP (& ALLOWING OTHERS TO HELP YOU)
- SPENDING QUALITY TIME (UNDISTRACTED)

"As soon as you trust yourself, you will know how to live."

- Johann Wolfgang von Goethe (German Writer, Poet, Creator)

MY TEAM

IT'S BEEN SAID THAT YOU ARE THE RESULT OF THE 5 PEOPLE YOU SPEND MOST
OF YOUR 'QUALITY' TIME WITH.
YOUR CLOSE RELATIONSHIPS HAVE A LARGE IMPACT ON YOUR LIFE.
THEY SHAPE YOUR PERSPECTIVE & WORLDVIEW IN REAL WAYS.
UNDERSTAND & APPRECIATE YOUR TEAM!

WHO ARE THE FIVE
MOST IMPORTANT
PEOPLE
IN MY LIFE?

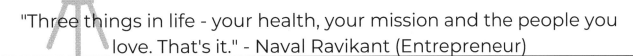

"Three things in life - your health, your mission and the people you
love. That's it." - Naval Ravikant (Entrepreneur)

MY EMOTIONAL INTELLIGENCE

EMOTIONAL INTELLIGENCE OR 'EQ' IS THE ABILITY TO BETTER REGULATE YOUR OWN EMOTIONS. CONSCIOUSLY UNDERSTANDING YOUR EMOTIONAL TRIGGERS & REACTIONS WILL BETTER ALLOW YOU TO EXERT MORE EMOTIONAL CONTROL. REACT THE WAY YOU INTEND!

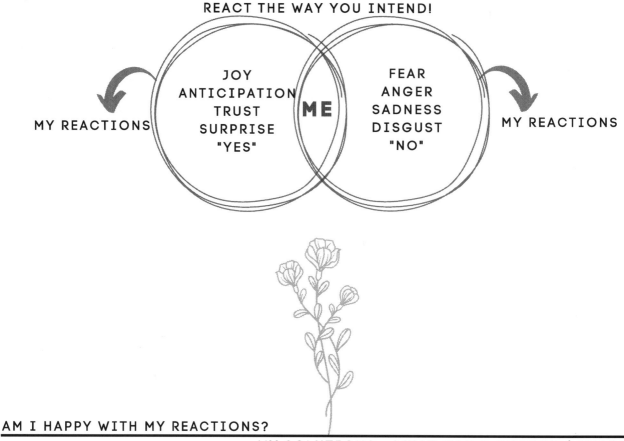

MY REACTIONS

JOY
ANTICIPATION
TRUST
SURPRISE
"YES"

ME

FEAR
ANGER
SADNESS
DISGUST
"NO"

MY REACTIONS

AM I HAPPY WITH MY REACTIONS?

MY SOLUTIONS - WHAT CAN I CHANGE / ADAPT?

TRY THESE TO INCREASE YOUR EQ:
- BECOME MORE SELF AWARE (WHAT YOU ARE DOING NOW;)
- BRING YOUR EMOTIONAL REACTIONS INTO YOUR CONSCIOUS AWARENESS
- RECALL YOUR REACTIONS - GOOD & BAD - WHAT CAN YOU DO DIFFERENTLY?
- RECONGNIZE YOUR TRIGGERS - WORDS / THINGS / PEOPLE
- TRY TO GIVE SPACE / TIME BETWEEN THE TRIGGER & YOUR REACTION
- BREATHE - 3 DEEP BREATHES - LONGER EXHALE (SEE 4-8-4 BREATHING)
- WILL YOU THINK THIS IS A GOOD REACTION TOMORROW?

"CEO's are hired for their intellect and business expertise - and fired for a lack of Emotional Intelligence."
- Daniel Goleman (Author - "Emotional Intelligence")

MY 8 EMOTIONAL WORLDS

UNDERSTANDING THE TRIGGERS OR STIMULUS WHICH SPARK YOUR EMOTIONS IS PERSONAL. EQUALLY, GETTING TO KNOW YOUR EMOTIONAL REACTIONS TO THAT STIMULUS IS IMPORTANT.
BE BETTER IN CONTROL OF YOUR EMOTIONAL WELL-BEING.

WHAT GIVES ME THIS EMOTION (STIMULI)   MY EMOTIONAL REACTIONS

JOY

TRUST

ANTICIPATION

SURPRISE

FEAR

ANGER

SADNESS

DISGUST

YOUR 8 EMOTIONS BASED ON THE "WHEEL OF EMOTIONS"
BY PYSCHOLOGY PROFESSOR ROBERT PLUTCHIK

"All these storms falling upon us are signs that the weather will soon clear and that things will go well for us. For neither good nor bad can last forever." - Miguel de Cervantes (Writer - "Don Quixote")

112

MY VULNERABILITIES

LOWERING MY DEFENSES FOR POSITIVE GROWTH

LOWERING DEFENSES TO ALLOW FOR GROWTH, FAILURE & EXPLORATION

VULNERABLE

INVULNERABLE

YOU KEEP EVERYTHING RISKY & POTENTIALLY HURTFUL OUT, NOTHING CAN HURT OR ATTACK YOU.

EXAMPLE

VULNERABILITY ALLOWS YOU TO EXPRESS YOURSELF AUTHENTICALLY; YOUR FEARS, HOPES, JOYS, PROBLEMS & DREAMS. IT'S NOT EASY & THERE ARE RISKS, YOU COULD STUMBLE, PEOPLE COULD LAUGH... BUT IF YOU ARE BEING YOUR TRUE-SELF, WHAT'S TO LAUGH AT? THE REWARDS ARE **GREAT**, IF YOU ARE WILLING TO TRY?

INVULNERABILITY SOUNDS GREAT, BUT IN REALITY, YOU ARE STUCK. YOU ARE GOING NOWHERE. YOU CAN'T RISK, TRY OR CREATE, AS THAT INVOLVES MAKING MISTAKES & LEARNING NEW THINGS. YOU ARE UNWILLING TO LEAVE YOUR COMFORT ZONE, SO LITTLE OR NO GROWTH CAN OCCUR.

WHERE DO I FEEL VULNERABLE?

EMOTIONAL, ECONOMIC, SOCIAL, PHYSICAL, INTELLECTUAL

WHAT'S HOLDING ME BACK?

HOW CAN I CREATE THE CONDITIONS TO EXPRESS MY TRUE FEELINGS?

VULNERABILITY IS YOUR STRENGTH, BECAUSE;
- YOU LOWER YOUR WALLS (NOT FORCING YOURSELF TO "OPEN UP").
- YOU'RE ABLE TO SHARE YOUR GENUINE FEELINGS.
- IT ALLOWS YOU TO BUILD INTIMACY.
- IT HOLDS THE KEY TO AUTHENTIC RELATIONSHIPS.
- IT BREAKS DOWN BARRIERS TO COMMUNICATION.
- IT REDUCES LONELINESS, AS YOU CAN TRULY CONNECT WITH OTHERS.
- IT HELPS YOU FIND WAYS TO LIVE YOUR OWN GREAT LIFE.

SOMETIMES IT'S TOO HARD TO WRITE IT DOWN. SO DON'T, THINK, SPEAK OR SING ABOUT IT

"Vulnerability is not winning or losing. It's having the courage to show up when you can't control the outcome."
- Brene Brown (Author, Speaker, Researcher)

MY INTIMATE MOMENTS

INTIMACY = MUTUAL VULNERABILITY, GENUINE OPENNESS,
SHARING, COMPANIONSHIP, TRUST & AUTHENTICITY.

MY EXPERIENTIAL INTIMACY   CREATE INTIMATE EXPERIENCES - BONDING ACTIVITES

MY EMOTIONAL INTIMACY   FEEL SAFE SHARING CLOSE, PERSONAL FEELINGS & EMOTIONS

MY INTELLECTUAL INTIMACY   COMFORTABLE SHARING IDEAS, BELIEFS & OPINIONS,
EVEN IF DISAGREE

"It is not time or opportunity that is to determine intimacy - it is disposition alone. seven years would be insufficient to make some people acquainted with each other, and seven days are more than enough for others." - Jane Austen (English Novelist)

MY LOVE LANGUAGES

HOW DO YOU (& YOUR PARTNER) EXPRESS LOVE?
WHAT ARE YOUR (& THEIR) NEEDS? KNOWING THIS & TAKING ACTION CAN HELP
ANY LOVING PARTNERSHIP. BASED ON "5 LOVE LANGUAGES" BY GARY CHAPMAN

"If I know what love is, it is because of you." - Hermann Hesse

QUALITY TIME　　　　CREATE MOMENTS & EXPERIENCES, SPEND FOCUSED TIME TOGETHER

WHAT IS YOUR RANKING
OF EACH 1 - 5?

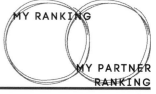

MY RANKING

MY PARTNER RANKING

PHYSICAL TOUCH　　　　TOUCH & PHYSICAL INTIMACY

MY RANKING

MY PARTNER RANKING

WORDS OF AFFIRMATION　　　ENCOURAGEMENT, APPRECIATION, LISTENING, EMPATHIZE

MY RANKING

MY PARTNER RANKING

RECIEVING GIFTS　　　　THOUGHTFUL GIFTS & GENUINE GESTURES

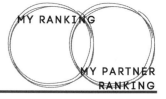

MY RANKING

MY PARTNER RANKING

ACTS OF SERVICE　　　DOING THOUGHTFUL ACTIONS, ACTIVELY HELPING THE OTHER

MY RANKING

MY PARTNER RANKING

"Love yourself first and everything else falls into line. You really
have to love yourself to get anything done in this world."
- Lucille Ball (American Actor & Producer)

MY SELF-TALK

THE GOOD

THE BAD & UGLY

NEGATIVE SELF TALK
- IDENTIFY IT WHEN IT HAPPENS
- MAKE IT CONSCIOUS
- UNDERSTAND WHY? REASONS
- TAKE CONTROL
- CHANGE PERSPECTIVE
- WRITE IT OUT

POSITIVE SOLUTIONS

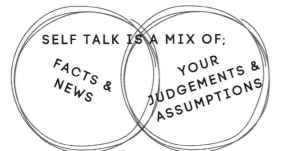

SELF TALK IS A MIX OF;

FACTS & NEWS

YOUR JUDGEMENTS & ASSUMPTIONS

THE NAME OF MY NEGATIVE ALTER-EGO IS:

IT CAN BE HELPFUL TO NAME YOUR INNER CRITIC,
IT CAN CREATE A SEPARATION IN YOUR HEAD.
WHEN YOUR NEGATIVE TALK KICKS IN;
RECOGNIZE IT, NAME IT & DECIDE TO LISTEN, OR NOT?
IF YOU GIVE IT POWER, IT WILL HAVE POWER OVER YOU!

MY HEARTBREAK & HEALING

"The soul would have no rainbow if the eyes had no tears."
- Native American Proverb

MY STAGES OF LOSS / GRIEF

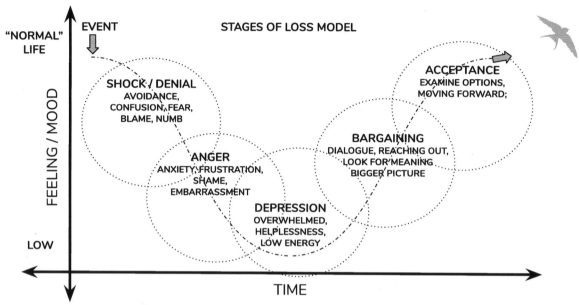

STAGES OF LOSS MODEL

"NORMAL" LIFE

EVENT

FEELING / MOOD

SHOCK / DENIAL
AVOIDANCE, CONFUSION, FEAR, BLAME, NUMB

ANGER
ANXIETY, FRUSTRATION, SHAME, EMBARRASSMENT

DEPRESSION
OVERWHELMED, HELPLESSNESS, LOW ENERGY

BARGAINING
DIALOGUE, REACHING OUT, LOOK FOR MEANING BIGGER PICTURE

ACCEPTANCE
EXAMINE OPTIONS, MOVING FORWARD;

LOW

TIME

THIS IS A MODEL ONLY - TO ALLOW YOU TO UNDERSTAND IT'S 'NORMAL' TO GO THROUGH STAGES AFTER LOSS. THESE WILL CHANGE OVER TIME & FOR THE INDIVIDUAL.

BASED ON THE KUBLER-ROSS MODEL - THE FIVE STAGES OF GRIEF

"What we have once enjoyed deeply we can never lose. All that we love deeply becomes part of us." - Helen Keller (Author, Inspiration)

HOW DO I PROCESS LOSS?   DO I IDENTIFY WITH ANY STAGES?

MY STRATEGIES THAT HELP

MAINTAINING HOPE IS KEY WHEN YOU'RE IN ANY STAGE OF LOSS/GRIEF. SEE "MY HOPE" PG.167

"Healing doesn't mean the damage ever existed. It means the damage no longer controls your life."
- Native American Proverb

117

"I can shake off everything as I write;
my sorrows disappear,
my courage is reborn."

- Anne Frank

THE DIARY OF ANNE FRANK IS ONE OF THE MOST INSPIRATIONAL DEPICTIONS
OF THE SIMPLE JOYS OF LIFE EVER TOLD.
WRITTEN DURING WWII BY A YOUNG JEWISH GERMAN-DUTCH GIRL, WHILE
LIVING IN HIDING IN AMSTERDAM. HER WORDS HAVE BEEN AN INSPIRATION TO
MILLIONS - EVEN IN THE HEART OF DARKNESS.

MY COMFORT ZONE

"A comfort zone is a beautiful place, but nothing grows there."
- Unknown

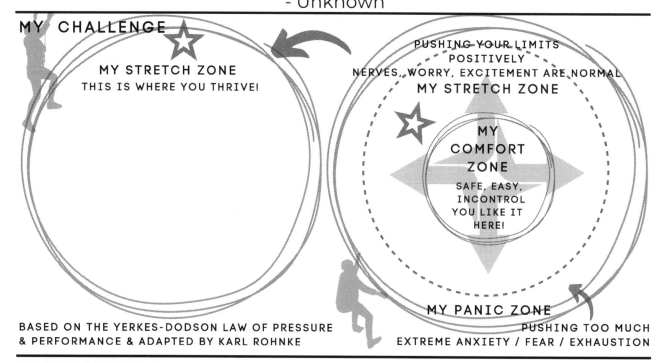

MY CHALLENGE

MY STRETCH ZONE
THIS IS WHERE YOU THRIVE!

PUSHING YOUR LIMITS
POSITIVELY
NERVES, WORRY, EXCITEMENT ARE NORMAL
MY STRETCH ZONE

MY COMFORT ZONE
SAFE, EASY, INCONTROL YOU LIKE IT HERE!

MY PANIC ZONE
PUSHING TOO MUCH
EXTREME ANXIETY / FEAR / EXHAUSTION

BASED ON THE YERKES-DODSON LAW OF PRESSURE & PERFORMANCE & ADAPTED BY KARL ROHNKE

MY REASONS WHY?

MY STRATEGIES

MY DESIRED OUTCOMES

"The mind stretched by new experience can never go back to its old dimensions." - Oliver Wendell Holmes Jr. (US Supreme Court Justice)

MY NORMAL

"I am not strange. I am just not normal."
- Salvador Dali (Spanish Surrealist Artist)

AM I NORMAL?

NORMAL   ECCENTRIC

ORDINARY   GENIUS

DO I WANT TO BE NORMAL?

NO, NOT AT ALL   YES, VERY MUCH

WHAT IS MY "NORMAL"?

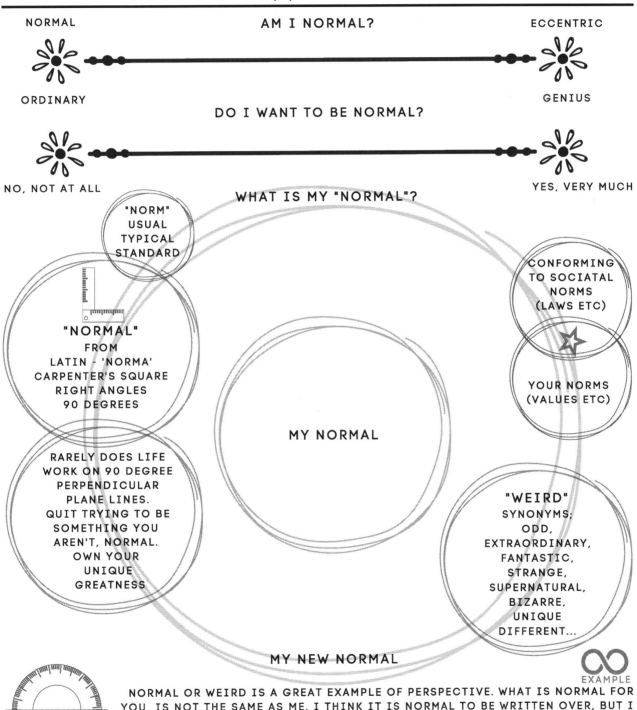

"NORM"
USUAL
TYPICAL
STANDARD

"NORMAL"
FROM
LATIN - 'NORMA'
CARPENTER'S SQUARE
RIGHT ANGLES
90 DEGREES

RARELY DOES LIFE
WORK ON 90 DEGREE
PERPENDICULAR
PLANE LINES.
QUIT TRYING TO BE
SOMETHING YOU
AREN'T, NORMAL.
OWN YOUR
UNIQUE
GREATNESS

MY NORMAL

CONFORMING
TO SOCIATAL
NORMS
(LAWS ETC)

YOUR NORMS
(VALUES ETC)

"WEIRD"
SYNONYMS;
ODD,
EXTRAORDINARY,
FANTASTIC,
STRANGE,
SUPERNATURAL,
BIZARRE,
UNIQUE
DIFFERENT...

MY NEW NORMAL

EXAMPLE

NORMAL OR WEIRD IS A GREAT EXAMPLE OF PERSPECTIVE. WHAT IS NORMAL FOR
YOU, IS NOT THE SAME AS ME. I THINK IT IS NORMAL TO BE WRITTEN OVER, BUT I
DOUBT THAT WOULD BE NORMAL FOR YOU? EMBRACE YOUR HEALTHY AB-NORMAL.

"If you are always trying to be normal you will never know how
amazing you can be."
Maya Angelou (American Poet, Writer, Civil Rights Activist)

MY SIX SENSES

YOUR FIVE SENSES ARE THE WAYS IN WHICH YOU INTERACT WITH THE PHYSICAL WORLD AROUND YOU. IT'S HOW YOU GATHER INFORMATION TO SURVIVE, YOUR SIXTH IS YOUR INTUITION, YOUR "GUT FEELING', IT TOO CAN KEEP YOU ALIVE!

SIGHT
WHAT I LIKE TO LOOK AT?

SOUND
WHAT I LIKE TO LISTEN TO & HEAR?

SMELL
WHAT I LIKE TO SMELL?

TASTE
WHAT FLAVOURS & TASTES I LIKE?

TOUCH
HOW I LIKE TO FEEL? BODILY SENSATIONS?

INTUITION
A FEELING OR INTERNAL REACTION TO STIMULATION YOU MAY OR MAY NOT KNOW ITS ORIGIN

- TUNE-IN (AWARENESS)
- FOCUS-IN (MEDITATE)
- WRITE-IT-OUT (PROCESS)
- ASK-QUESTIONS (UNDERSTAND)
- QUIET-TIME (CONTEMPLATE)
- TRUST-YOURSELF (EXPERIENCE)

"It's the beauty within us that makes it possible for us to recognize the beauty around us. The question is not what you look at but what you see." - Henry David Thoreau (Writer, Naturalist, Philosopher)

MY HABITS

"HABIT" - A SETTLED OR REGULAR TENDENCY OR PRACTICE,
ESPECIALLY ONE THAT IS HARD TO GIVE UP.
YOUR HABITS MAKE UP YOUR LIFE... ON REPLAY - BACK TO CIRCLES!

MY GOOD HABITS   WHY THEY WORK FOR ME?

MY BAD HABITS   MY ROAD TO CHANGE
THE ONES I WANT TO KEEP?   WHY DO I WANT THIS CHANGE?
                                                  WHAT ARE THE BENEFITS TO ME?
                                                  WHAT ARE THE BENEFITS TO OTHERS?
                                                  WHAT ARE THE FLOW-ON EFFECTS?
                                                  HOW WILL THIS MAKE ME FEEL?
                                                  DO I HAVE THE COURAGE TO MAKE A DECISION?

THE ONES I WANT TO CHANGE?

WHAT IS THE FIRST STEP TO CHANGE?

"It isn't the mountains ahead that wear you out, it's the pebble in your shoe" - Muhammad Ali ("the Greatest" - Boxing Legend)

MY TRIGGERS

"TRIGGER" - CAUSE AN EVENT OR SITUATION TO HAPPEN OR EXIST.
TRIGGERS ARE THE STIMULI TO ACT ON YOUR HABITS, YOUR HABITS THEN LEAD
TO CONSEQUENCES - THE GOOD & THE NOT-SO-MUCH

CONSEQUENCES WHAT DO YOU WANT TO CHANGE?	HABIT WHAT DO YOU DO?	TRIGGER(S) STIMULUS

∞ EXAMPLE   I CAN'T GET OVER MY EX | I THINK ABOUT MY EX | I SEE MY EX ON INSTAGRAM

TAKING ACTION

WANT TO CHANGE?
- KNOW YOUR CUES
- REMOVE / REDUCE SENSE CUES (SIGHT, SOUNDS ETC)
- FOCUS ON WHY THE CHANGE IS NEEDED
- VISUALIZE THE RESULTS AND BENEFITS
- GET SUPPORT
- PREPARE FOR SETBACKS
- REPLACE THE HABIT (WITH A BETTER ONE)
- MAKE IT SUSTAINABLE - GOALS ARE GREAT BUT AIM FOR LONG-TERM

"Next in importance to having a good aim is to recognize when to pull the Trigger." - David Letterman (US Late Night TV Icon)

MY RITUALS

RITUALS COME FROM RELIGIOUS "RITES";
CEREMONIES CONSISTING OF A SERIES OF ACTIONS IN A PRESCRIBED ORDER.
TODAY, YOU LIKELY HAVE YOUR OWN RITUALS, YOUR OWN PROCESSES YOU GO
THROUGH ON A DAILY BASIS. DO THEY WORK FOR YOU?

WHAT IS IT?	DOES IT WORK FOR ME?	CHANGE IT UP?
MORNING		
DAY		
 EVENING / NIGHT		

∞ EXAMPLE I WAKE UP, SWITCH ON MY PHONE, READ THE NEWS, GET UP...

THWART HEDONISTIC ADAPTATION (GETTING BORED WITH STUFF /
ROUTINES). CHANGE IT UP. SOME SIMPLE TWEAKS & ADJUSTMENTS CAN
KEEP THINGS INTERESTING

MY GOALS / OUTCOMES

"Stand for something or you will fall for anything.
Today's mighty oak is yesterday's nut that held its
ground."
- Rosa Parks

SOCIAL

Humans are social animals. Chances are, that is not news to you. Humans have survived and thrived, not because of physical strength, but because of cooperation. By working together, the human race grew a collective strength.

Working with each other allows for specialized roles (work). You can rely on others to provide the goods and services that you cannot provide yourself (that's where money comes in). Society is a collective, which means to co-operate with others to get all the needed resources, while allowing others to do the same.

Your Social World is one of interaction and connection with those around you. You may be strong and independent but that doesn't mean you don't need other people. Everyone needs to socialize and you too need personal connections to thrive.

Your social health will impact your physical health in a very real way. A lack of social connection can be more harmful than some of the more typically unhealthy behaviours, such as smoking or lack of exercise. Being accepted as part of a wider social group gives you belonging. Social isolation is not new, but it is increasing, especially with the move away from real-world interaction to virtual ones.

Communication is a major part of your Social World. How you communicate is vital for the success of your social connections. Your communication matters and the more you understand your own habits and style, the more you will be better at adapting these to the people and situations around you.

Communication is about correctly understanding those around you, and those around you correctly understanding you. Effective communication and respectful communication will be a great aid in developing a fulfilling social life. This impacts your personal and professional life, as well as your overall well-being.

Humans have created thousands of methods to communicate. At last count, there were about 6500 languages used on Earth to share information. Considering there are only about 195 countries on the planet, the diversity in language shows how humans have had the need and desire to interact, no matter the culture or circumstance.

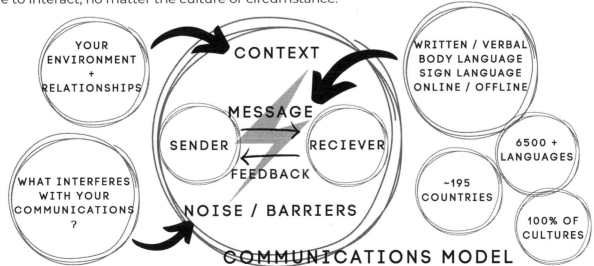

SOCIAL

In this section, you'll be looking at the most important social connections to you. It's important to maintain and prioritize your key social connections. Relationships take effort, all relationships, and if you want them to flourish, you'd better make sure you are putting in the effort too.

It's not about the number of social interactions and friends you have, it's the quality of these interactions and friendships that matter. Being everyone's friend is an impossible goal.

Friendship is two-way. Ask yourself, how many people will you drop everything for in a time of need? Are your friends there for you throughout good times and bad? Are you there for them? Knowing who is really there for you, and being there for them will cultivate deeper and more meaningful connections. Friendship is one of the greatest joys in human life. It's a trusted, fulfilling, mutually rewarding relationship like no other.

DUNBARS SOCIAL NUMBERS.

RESEARCH SUGGESTS YOUR BRAIN CAN ONLY HANDLE SO MANY PEOPLE, NAMES & FACES.

- 5 CLOSE / BEST FRIENDS (YOUR KIN)
- 15 GOOD FRIENDS (YOUR EXTENDED FAMILY)
- 50 FRIENDS (YOUR WIDER CIRCLE)
- 150 - THE MAXIMUM NUMBER YOU CAN MAINTAIN MEANINGFUL RELATIONSHIPS WITH (YOUR TRIBE)
- 500 - ACQUAINTANCES (YOUR NEIGHBOURHOOD)
- 1500 - FACE AND NAME RECOGNITION (YOUR KNOWN WORLD)

ROBIN DUNBAR
(ANTHROPOLOGIST)

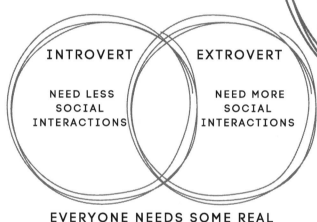

INTROVERT — NEED LESS SOCIAL INTERACTIONS

EXTROVERT — NEED MORE SOCIAL INTERACTIONS

EVERYONE NEEDS SOME REAL INTERACTIONS

Dunbar's numbers are to demonstrate, you can't be everyone's friend, you can be kind, polite and helpful to everyone, but you have a limited capacity for truly meaningful relationships.

The number of people you need around you is personal. Another thing that will impact your social needs is how intro/extroverted you are. Some people need more people around them, while others are happy with just a few.

The concept of 'friends' has changed since Facebook. Now a "friend" can be someone you meet once at a party or conference, or have never met at all. But are they actual friends? Once again, it's you who decides who is a friend, foe and someone who is not worth your time.

As the other part of cultivating healthy relationships is also letting some go. Toxic relationships will cause you significant harm. Manipulation, deceit, narcissism. As you are changing through your own life-course, it's natural and normal for the people around you to change too. The people you chose to spend your time with have a large influence over your life. Choose wisely, and never forget the value and responsibility of true friendship.

MY GROUPS & ALLIANCES

BUILDING MY PERSONAL & PROFESSIONAL RELATIONSHIPS THROUGH NETWORKING (MEETING NEW PEOPLE)

CREATE NEW ALLIANCES

HOW TO EXPAND MY NETWORK?
- JOIN A PROFESSIONAL ORGANIZATION (WORK OR INTEREST)
- VOLUNTEER
- CONTACT ALUMNI (SCHOOL/COLLEGE/WORK)
- REFERRALS FROM CURRENT NETWORK
- ATTEND EVENTS - HOST EVENTS (VIRTUAL OR INPERSON)
- GO WHERE "SUCCESS" GOES (WHATEVER THAT MEANS TO YOU)
- EXPLORE A NEW INTEREST (BREAK YOUR MOULD)
- ADAPT A GIVING ATTITUDE - HELPING OTHERS WILL HELP YOU
- BE AUTHENTIC - BRING YOUR BEST SELF
- NERVES ARE NORMAL - BUTTERFLIES IN FORMATION
- FOLLOW UP - ACTIONS SPEAK LOUDER THAN WORDS...
- BUT... POLITE, REPSECTFUL & INSIGHTFUL WORDS WILL ALWAYS HELP YOU ON YOUR WAY

ACTIVITIES & EVENTS TO SHARE

HOW WILL I MAKE TIME FOR FAMILY & FRIENDS? →

"Don't compare yourself to others. There is no comparison between the sun & the moon. They both shine when it's their time" - Unknown

MY KEY GROUPS & PEOPLE

GROUP / PERSON	HOW I WILL CREATE QUALITY TIME WITH THEM

"The meaning of life is to find your gift. The purpose of life is to give it away." - William Shakespeare (English Playwright - Poet)

MY CELEBRATION CALANDAR

SPECIAL DAYS, ANNIVERSARIES & PEOPLE

JANUARY	FEBRUARY	MARCH
APRIL	MAY	JUNE
JULY	AUGUST	SEPTEMBER
OCTOBER	NOVEMBER	DECEMBER

"If you want to go fast, go alone. If you want to go far, go together." - African Proverb

MY COMMUNITY

A COMMUNITY IS A SOCIAL UNIT (A GROUP OF LIVING THINGS) WITH COMMONALITY, SUCH AS; NORMS, VALUES, CUSTOMS, OR PLACE. MEMBERS OF COMMUNITIES RELY ON EACH OTHER AS A SOCIAL NETWORK FOR SECURITY, ECONOMIC & SOCIAL NEEDS.

MY COMMUNITY GROUPS

HOW CAN I CONTRIBUTE TO MY COMMUNITY?

MY POTENTIAL NEW COMMUNITY GROUPS

WHAT INTERESTS / HOBBIES / GROUPS DO I IDENTIFY?

FESTIVALS AND CELEBRATIONS TO SHARE

"We build too many walls and not enough bridges."
- Isaac Newton (Physicist, Astronomer, Mathematician)

MY RIGHTS & RESPONSIBILITIES

WE ALL HAVE RIGHTS - AS A HUMAN & CITIZEN, GLOBAL OR COUNTRY, KNOW
YOUR RIGHTS & ENSURE THEY ARE RESPECTED - BE ASSERTIVE!
EQUALLY, WE ALL HAVE RESPONSIBILITIES - TO OURSELVES & OTHERS -
UNDERSTAND YOUR RESPONSIBILITIES & LIVE UP TO THEM.

STAND UP FOR MYSELF & OTHERS	LIVE WITH INTEGRITY
MY RIGHTS	MY RESPONSIBILITIES

&

"Think for yourself and let the others enjoy the privilege of doing so too." - Voltaire (French Enlightenment Philosopher, Writer)

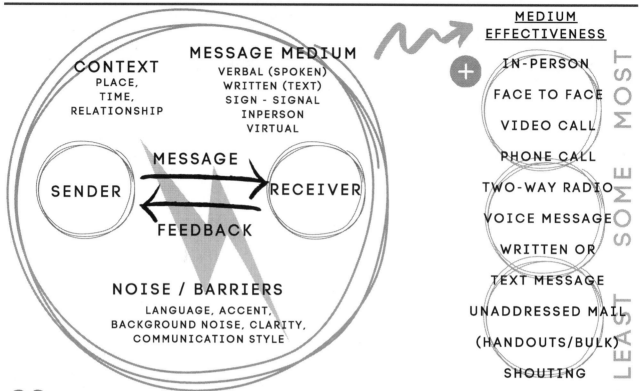

CONTEXT
PLACE,
TIME,
RELATIONSHIP

MESSAGE MEDIUM
VERBAL (SPOKEN)
WRITTEN (TEXT)
SIGN - SIGNAL
INPERSON
VIRTUAL

MESSAGE

SENDER → RECEIVER

FEEDBACK

NOISE / BARRIERS
LANGUAGE, ACCENT,
BACKGROUND NOISE, CLARITY,
COMMUNICATION STYLE

MEDIUM
EFFECTIVENESS

IN-PERSON
FACE TO FACE
VIDEO CALL
PHONE CALL
TWO-WAY RADIO
VOICE MESSAGE
WRITTEN OR
TEXT MESSAGE
UNADDRESSED MAIL
(HANDOUTS/BULK)
SHOUTING

MOST ... SOME ... LEAST

∞ EXAMPLE WHY? EFFECTIVENESS DROPS WITH LACK OF CONTEXT & NON VERBAL CUES (BODY LANGUAGE, TONE ETC) ALSO, HOW QUICKLY ONE RECEIVES FEEDBACK? IS IT IMMEDIATE OR DELAYED?

WHAT ARE YOUR BARRIERS TO BETTER UNDERSTAND - BE UNDERSTOOD?
WHAT CAN I DO ABOUT THESE BARRIERS?

DO I PROVIDE APPROPRIATE FEEDBACK - RESPONSE?

WHAT IS YOUR PREFERRED MEDIUM FOR COMMUNICATION?
WHY? IS IT EFFECTIVE FOR MY NEEDS?

"Communication - the human connection - is the key to personal and career success." - Paul J. Meyer (Author, Coach)

MY COMMUNICATION STYLE

HOW DO I TYPICALLY
COMMUNICATE?

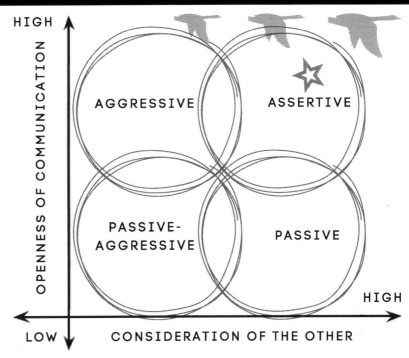

OPENNESS OF COMMUNICATION MEANS BEING DIRECT & CLEAR ABOUT YOUR MESSAGE.
CONSIDERATION OF OTHER IS TO LISTEN & RECEIVE WITH RESPECT, CURIOSITY & OPENNESS.
BE ASSERTIVE - COMMUNICATE CLEARLY & RESPECTFULLY WITH CONFIDENCE & CONTROL

MY COMMUNICATION HABITS

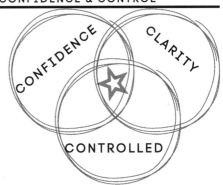

MY COMMUNICATIONS SOLUTIONS

"BE KIND, for everyone you meet is fighting a HARD battle."
- Socrates (~399BC - Founder of Western Moral Philosophy)

MY CONFLICT

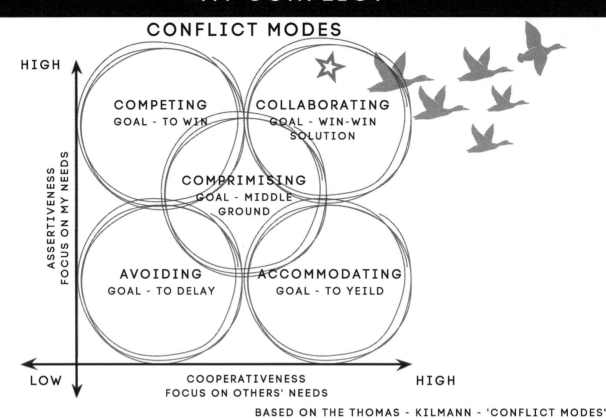

CONFLICT MODES

COMPETING
GOAL - TO WIN

COLLABORATING
GOAL - WIN-WIN
SOLUTION

COMPRIMISING
GOAL - MIDDLE
GROUND

AVOIDING
GOAL - TO DELAY

ACCOMMODATING
GOAL - TO YEILD

HIGH

ASSERTIVENESS
FOCUS ON MY NEEDS

LOW

COOPERATIVENESS
FOCUS ON OTHERS' NEEDS

HIGH

BASED ON THE THOMAS - KILMANN - 'CONFLICT MODES'

HOW DO I HANDLE CONFLICT?

MY RULES FOR CONFLICT RESOLUTION

REDUCE IMMEDIATE TENSION
IMPROVE ACCURACY OF INFORMATION FOR BOTH SIDES
LIMIT THE NUMBER OF ISSUES - FOCUS
AGREE ON GROUND RULES
EXPLORE ALTERNATIVES / OPTIONS
SEE IT FROM THEIR VIEWPOINT - PERSPECTIVE
SEEK COMMON GROUND TO BUILD UPON
MAINTAIN RESPECT
KEEP COOL - GET SOME AIR

"Whenever you are in conflict with someone, there is one factor that can make the difference between damaging your relationship and deepening it. That factor is attitude."
- Ramachandra (Hero of the "Ramayana" - Hindu Deity)

MY CLEAR COMMUNICATION

GET TO WHERE YOU WANT TO GO, FASTER, THROUGH DELIVERING A CLEAR
MESSAGE. BASED ON THE 7 C'S OF EFFECTIVE COMMUNICATION.

HOW CAN I IMPROVE MY COMMUNICATIONS?

CLEAR
AVOID COMPLEX WORDS & PHRASES - JARGON

CONCISE
BE SPECIFIC - NOT VAGUE

CONCRETE
GET TO THE POINT - NOT OVERLY WORDY

CORRECT
USE CORRECT TERMS, FACTS & GRAMMAR

COMPLETE
IS THE MESSAGE COMPLETE?

COHERENT
DOES THE MESSAGE MAKE SENSE? LOGIC? FLOW?

COURTEOUS
ENSURE THE MESSAGE IS POLITE & TACTFUL

"Free speech carries with it some freedom to listen."
- Bob Marley (Singer, Songwriter, Reggae Legend)

136

MY CULTURAL COMMUNICATIONS

YOUR CULTURAL BACKGROUND IMPACTS THE WAY YOU COMMUNICATE. EVEN IF YOU SPEAK THE SAME LANGAUGE, THERE ARE STILL MANY DETAILED COMPONENTS THAT MAKE HUMAN COMMUNICATION. BY UNDERSTANDING YOUR STYLE, YOU CAN BETTER UNDERSTAND THOSE AROUND YOU & ADAPT TO BE MOST EFFECTIVE.

WHERE DO YOU IDENTIFY? WHERE DOES THE OTHER?

MY CULTURAL COMMUNICATION STYLE

COLLECTIVIST — **INDIVIDUALISTIC**

COLLECTIVIST INDIVIDUAL

INDIVIDUAL COLLECTIVIST

- WE ARE INTER-DEPENDENT
- WORKING FOR GROUP GOALS
- FAMILY & COMMUNITY FOCUS
- MAINTAIN GROUP RESPECT

- I AM INDEPENDENT
- WORKING FOR MY OWN GOALS
- SELF FOCUS
- MAINTAIN SELF RESPECT

INDIRECT — **DIRECT**

- IMPLICIT - NON VERBAL
- RELATIONSHIPS ESSENTIAL
- GREATER AMBIGUITY
- CONFORMITY IS EXPECTED
- UNDERSTANDING NORMS REQUIRED

- EXPLICIT - VERBAL
- WORDS & MESSAGE ESSENTIAL
- WHAT IS SAID IS WHAT IS MEANT
- DISAGREEMENT IS OKAY
- DETAILS OFTEN PROVIDED

"IMPLY" FOLD INWARDS INTWINED

IMPLICIT — **EXPLICIT**

"EXPLICATE" FOLD OUTWARDS UNFOLD

IMPLIED THOUGH NOT PLAINLY EXPRESSED LESS DETAILS PROVIDED NEED TO UNDERSTAND CONTEXT

∞ EXAMPLE

STATED CLEARLY; IN DETAIL LEAVING LITTLE ROOM FOR CONFUSION OR DOUBT CONTEXT HAS LESS IMPORTANCE

ADAPTED BY WORK AND RESEARCH OF DUTCH SOCIAL PSYCHOLOGIST, GEERT HOFSTEDE

MY POWER DISTANCE
HOW EASY CAN YOU SAY "NO" TO POWER?

HIGH-POWER DISTANCE — **LOW-POWER DISTANCE**

- POWER IS AUTHORITATIVE & STRICT
- HARDER TO ACCESS AUTHORITY
- HIERARCHY IS HEAVY
- CANNOT OPENLY DISAGREE
- RESPECT OF RANK / TRADTION

- POWER IS MORE DISTRIBUTED
- EASIER TO ACCESS AUTHORITY
- HIERARCHY IS FLAT
- DISAGREEMENTS ACCEPTABLE
- RESPECT OF PERFORMANCE / EFFORT

"We have two ears and one mouth so that we can listen twice as much as we speak." - Epictetus (Greek Philosopher)

MY EMPATHY

EMPATHY IS FEELING WHAT ANOTHER PERSON IS FEELING. YOU PUT YOURSELF
IN 'THEIR SHOES' TO REALLY UNDERSTAND.
EMPATHY STARTS WITH BEING A BETTER LISTENER.

HOW CAN I BE A BETTER LISTENER?

FOCUS ON THE SPEAKER
AVOID DISTRACTIONS
BODY LANGUAGE TO SHOW YOU FOLLOW / CARE
ASK THOUGHTFUL QUESTIONS
ALLOW FOR ANSWERS
DON'T ASSUME YOU KNOW
TRY NOT TO INTERRUPT (OR FINISH SENTENCES)
CLARIFY AS NEEDED - REPHRASE TO ENSURE UNDERSTANDING
ALLOW FOR SILENCE
YOU'RE NOT THERE TO SOLVE ALL THEIR PROBLEMS - JUST LISTEN

HOW CAN I LEARN MORE ABOUT OTHERS?

STAYING CURIOUS & OPEN-MINEDED

QUESTIONING MY ASSUMPTIONS

WHEN YOU ASSUME, YOU DON'T ALLOW THE OTHER TO BE THEMSELVES.
QUESTIONING YOUR ASSUMPTIONS WILL HELP YOU FIND GENUINE
CONNECTIONS WITH OTHERS & HELP YOU FIND GREATER PATHWAYS
TO WHOM YOU MAY HAVE MISUNDERSTOOD IN THE PAST.

"ASSUME"
(VERB) =
SUPPOSED TO BE
THE CASE,
WITHOUT
PROOF

ELEPHANTS ARE KNOWN TO BE THE MOST
EMPATHETIC IN THE ANIMAL KINGDOM

EMPATHY HAS GREAT VALUE TO BOTH PARTIES,
BUT SOMETIMES THIS CAN BE PAINFUL.
IF EMPATHY ISN'T THE ANSWER, TRY COMPASSION..

"Learning to stand in somebody else's shoes, to see through their
eyes, that's how peace begins. And it's up to you to make that
happen. Empathy is a quality of character that can change the world."
- Barack Obama (44th President of the USA)

MY COMPASSION

COMPASSION IS THE FEELING OF CONCERN FOR ANOTHER'S SUFFERING & A REAL DESIRE TO HELP. IT COMES FROM THE LATIN ROOT FOR "CO-SUFFERING" OR "TO SUFFER TOGETHER"

SELF-COMPASSION

HOW CAN I BE MORE COMPASSIONATE TOWARDS MYSELF?
BEING KIND TO YOURSELF WHEN BEING CONFRONTED WITH PERSONAL SHORTCOMINGS & MISTAKES

 EXAMPLE TAKE SOME OF YOUR OWN ADVICE; WHAT WOULD SAY TO A GOOD FRIEND IN YOUR SITUATION? PRACTICE THAT ON YOURSELF. WOULD YOU CALL YOUR FRIEND 'A LOSER' FOR FAILING OR MAKING A MISTAKE?

COMPASSION TOWARDS OTHERS

HOW CAN I BE MORE COMPASSIONATE?

COMPASSION IS SEEN AS ONE OF THE HIGHEST VIRTUES IN HUMANITY; EASTERN & WESTERN PHILOSOPHIES, GLOBAL RELIGIONS, HUMAN RIGHTS LEGISLATION & ETHICAL FRAMEWORKS ALL HAVE IT DEEPLY ROOTED IN THEIR DOGMAS & TEACHINGS.

"A new command I give you: Love one another. As I have loved you, so you must love one another."
- Jesus Christ

"Compassion is the wish to see others free from suffering."
-14th Dalai Lama

"You will never enter paradise until you have faith and you will not complete your faith until you love one another."
- Prophet Muhammad (Peace Be Upon Him)

"One, remember to look up at the stars and not down at your feet.
Two, never give up work.
Work gives you meaning and purpose and life is empty without it.
Three, if you are lucky enough to find love, remember it is there and don't throw it away."

- Stephen Hawking

ME, MYSELF AND I

SOLITUDE VERSUS LONELINESS

WHEN YOU'RE IN SOLITUDE, YOU'RE ALONE, PHYSICALLY - WHERE YOU CAN ENJOY YOUR OWN TIME. LONELINESS ON THE OTHERHAND CAN TAKE PLACE IN A CROWDED ROOM. IT'S THE FEELING OF HAVING NO ONE TO CONNECT WITH, NO ONE WHO REALLY SEES YOU, NOR UNDERSTANDS.

POSITIVE SOLITUDE

WHAT DO I LOVE TO DO WHILE ALONE?

NEGATIVE SOLITUDE

WHY DON'T I ENJOY BEING ALONE?

ENJOYING MY OWN TIME

NOT ENJOYING BEING ALONE

COMPANIONSHIP

LONELINESS

FEELING I HAVE PEOPLE TO CONNECT WITH*

FEELING I HAVE NO ONE TO CONNECT WITH*

*CONNECT WITH = GENUINE CONNECTION

HOW DO I FEEL WHEN I AM LONELY?

WHEN DO I FEEL LONELY?

MY STRATEGIES WHEN I FEEL LONELY?

IF YOU ARE LONELY:
- ACKNOWLEDGE IT
- PINPOINT YOUR EMOTIONS
- CULTIVATE GRATITUDE
- INITIATE DIALOG WITH FAMILY / FRIENDS
- REACH OUT TO OTHERS
- TRY NEW ACTIVITIES / SKILLS
- TRY A FOCUS SHIFT - AIM FOR LARGER LIFE GOALS
- FIND THINGS THAT INSPIRE / AWE
- HELP SOMEONE ELSE
- VOLUNTEER YOUR TIME
- CAN I CHANGE MY PERSPECTIVE?

CULTIVATING MOMENTS OF SOLITUDE

CULTIVATING SOLITUDE
- BEING ALONE MAY FEEL UNCOMFORTABLE AT FIRST
  - DON'T REACH FOR YOUR PHONE
- SIT, WALK, LIE DOWN - FEEL PHYSICALLY COMFORTABLE
- GO OUTSIDE IF YOU FEEL SAFE & SECURE TO DO SO
- RELAX - BREATHE
- UNDERSTAND - IT'S OK TO DO NOTHING SOMETIMES
- FOCUS ON MEANING - NATURE - YOUR LIFE GOALS
- SEE IT AS A PRECIOUS GIFT TO CONNECT WITH YOURSELF
- CREATE "SACRED SPACES" TO ENJOY YOUR ALONE TIME

"The whole value of solitude depends on oneself, it may be a sanctuary or a prison, a haven or a hell, as we ourselves make it."
- Sir John Lubbock (1st Baron Avebury, Writer "Peace & Happiness")

MY SUPERHERO

YOUR HERO CAN HELP YOU DECIDE WHAT YOU WOULD DO, IF YOU COULD DO ANYTHING? HOW WOULD YOU ACT? WHAT WOULD YOU LOVE TO DO? WHAT IS YOUR SUPERPOWER?

MY COSTUME & COLOURS

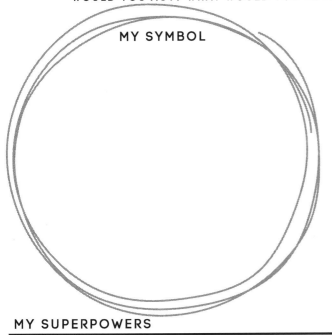

MY SYMBOL

MY SUPERPOWERS

WHAT I STAND FOR

MY ARCH-NEMISIS & CHALLENGES TO OVERCOME

FROM ANCIENT GREEK "HĒRŌS" - HERO- "PROTECTOR" OR "DEFENDER"

MY HEROS & GURUS

"HERO"
A REAL PERSON OR A FICTIONAL CHARACTER WHO, IN THE FACE OF DANGER OR EXTREME ADVERSITY - FIGHTS ON THROUGH FEATS OF INGENUITY, COURAGE & STRENGTH.

"GURU"
IS A SANSKRIT TERM FOR A TEACHER, GUIDE, EXPERT, OR MASTER, OF CERTAIN KNOWLEDGE OR FIELD.

YOUR HERO OR GURU IS ALSO YOUR GUIDE.
THEY WILL IMPACT YOUR VALUES & SHAPE YOUR WORLDVIEW.

MY REAL LIFE HEROS   HOW DO I RELATE?   MY FICTIONAL HEROS

MY TEACHERS / GUIDES & GURUS
HOW & WHY DOES THEIR MESSAGE IMPACT ME?

HOW DO MY HEROS / GURUS INSPIRE ME?

"I think a hero is an ordinary individual who finds strength to persevere and endure in spite of overwhelming obstacles."
- Christopher Reeve (the Original "Superman")

MENTAL

MY GOALS / OUTCOMES

"Iron rusts from disuse; water loses its purity from stagnation... even so does inaction sap the vigor of the mind."
- Leonardo da Vinci

MENTAL

Your Mental World is the control-center of this whole operation called Life. It has a massive impact on all your other worlds. Your brain is a key part of your decision-making processes and motivations, as well as the thoughts you have and the emotions they trigger. It's an important and complicated world.

By better understanding your mental world, you give yourself the power to make better decisions and have more thoughtful reactions. A big change your mental world has had to cope with, has been to that of the modern world. Your mind and brain have had to adapt quickly to these modern cultural and technological changes, but evolution takes time. Your world of focus has not had the chance to properly evolve into handling so much information and so much stimulation. Modern conveniences have made life easier, but not necessarily better; especially for the human brain. It's your mental world that has had to bear the brunt of these changes.

Globally, there have been increases in anxiety, depression and the decline in general mental health in the human population. Based on my experiences, as a book who has been around, one big factor has been the quick changeover in the way you humans now interact. Quality has switched to quantity, you're always connected, yet not. Your modern life has given many of you new habits, new worlds and new ways to share, but I have seen, if these aren't managed thoughtfully and in balance, there are very serious consequences. I'm not being a jealous book either! I know, I'm "old school", I love my online e-book friends. I just love being a book, you know and being handled and flipped through, I'm real, tangible, in your hands. Oh! Now I'm **blushing**. Moving on!

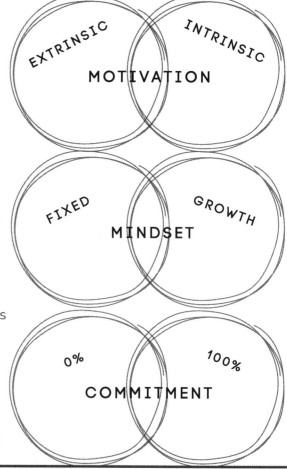

Making decisions is one important area you rely on your mental capacity for. Bad decisions mean you have to then suffer the consequences. No one likes regret, but you are the result of your decisions (and those who make decisions on your behalf). The key is ensuring your decisions align with the larger values and push you on the path towards your mission.

Choice is part of the decision making process, sometimes you have them, sometimes it feels you don't. Choice is another big mental paradox. Humans love to feel like they have choice, but too much is overwhelming. Choosing one colour out of five is easy, choosing one out of a thousand, not so much.

While your intelligence and knowledge are part of this world, it's not the main focus here. The brain is very much at the center of learning and discovery, but information alone doesn't translate into change, nor action. It's what you do with the information that matters. The focus in the mental world is of your mindset, motivations, fears and resilience. It's about your mental reactions and whether these are optimal for the life you want to live.

MENTAL

Your brain is a great computer. It's efficient and it automates functions, which is to your benefit. Imagine if you had to think about every step you took? But sometimes your brain works too efficiently and automates things which are not in your best interest.

Like you, your brain likes shortcuts. It finds ways to speed up processing and decision-making, especially for things it does regularly. These habits are on auto-pilot and will change little until there is either; 'The Crash', when the tipping point is reached, or you make a conscious decision to change. By making things conscious you're taking them out of the unconscious, you're deciding to exert more direct control, this is a mental challenge.

Your perspective is part of your conscious world. Whether you share it with others or not, you have a perspective. It's your mental ability to look at things from multiple viewpoints and weigh-up the information, then determine your own conclusions. That's the gift of your human brain. Diverse and differing perspectives are the birthplace of creativity and that's the birthplace of everything.

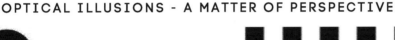

OPTICAL ILLUSIONS - A MATTER OF PERSPECTIVE

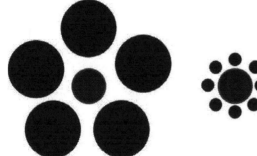

WHICH CENTER CIRCLE IS LARGER?   ARE THE HORIZONTAL LINES PARALLEL?

Your perspective is not fixed, it can change with new facts, but it can also be reinforced with complimentary information. It's shaped by those you listen to and identify with. In this section you are going to hone your perspective, develop it and understand it deeper.

Both fear and excitement can feel almost the same physically, but your perspective tells you they are different. The ability to change your perspective can really change everything; your reactions, your fears, your worries, your relationships and your life.

Your motivation to change, your will to continue and your reaction to failure, these will be much larger determinants of your success than simply the knowledge you possess. You may know movement is good for you, but that doesn't mean you have the motivation to do anything about it. Knowledge alone doesn't change anything unless it's somehow acted upon, or at least, passed on. Although your brain is yours, it may feel like you exert little influence over it. Will-power, determination, perseverance, are all mental, and none are easy.

One of the most incredible things about you, as a human, is your adaptability. You have the capacity to change and to adapt when situations change, you can and will find new ways and new solutions to your problems, although you will worry otherwise.
Here you tap into your mental potential.
Answers - Both circles are the same size; and yes, those are parallel lines.

MENTAL
MY INNER FOCUS & ATTITUDE

WHAT DO I ENJOY TO FOCUS ON?

HOW IS MY GENERAL ATTITUDE?

ATTITUDE
COMES FROM THE LATIN ROOT "POSTURE" OR "POSITION". IT'S YOUR DEFAULT "LIFE-POSITION" YOUR POINT OF VIEW, YOUR WAY OF THINKING.

WHAT ARE THE THINGS I LIKE TO SPEND TIME ON? WHAT IS IT ABOUT THEM THAT I ENJOY?

MY MENTAL FRUSTRATIONS

MY MENTAL TACTICS

WHAT ARE THE THINGS THAT ANNOY ME? SOMETIMES LITTLE THINGS. WHAT'S HOLDING ME BACK?

WHAT HAS PROVEN TO WORK FOR ME? MY TACTICS TO MOVE FORWARD HOW I STAY RESILIENT & HOPEFUL

YOU DON'T NEED TO WRITE IT DOWN OF COURSE. BUT AT LEAST THINK ABOUT IT... HONESTLY. DEVELOPING YOUR SELF-AWARENESS IS A KEY STEP IN UNDERSTANDING YOUR MOTIVATIONS & BEING THE BEST TRUE-BLUE YOU! (OR WHATEVER COLOUR YOU CHOOSE!)

MY GREAT EXPECTATIONS

YOUR EXPECTATIONS ARE VERY IMPORTANT. YOU WILL JUDGE REAL EVENTS, NOT ON THE EVENT ITSELF, BUT ON YOUR EXPECTATIONS OF IT. DISAPPOINTMENT, SURPRISE, JOY & ANGER ARE EMOTIONAL REACTIONS TO WHAT YOU EXPECT WILL HAPPEN.

OPTIMIST - "MY GLASS IS HALF-FULL"
WHAT MAKES ME OPTIMISTIC?
WHEN I LOOK AT THE POSITIVE SIDE?

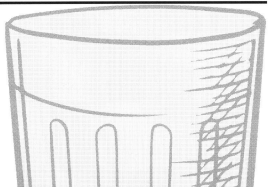

ANTICIPATION IS A GREAT WAY TO FEEL EXCITED ABOUT YOUR LIFE.
LOOKING FORWARD TO AN EVENT OR A FUTURE IS POSITIVE & REWARDING
KEEP YOUR EXPECTATIONS REALISTIC - BUT EXCITED ABOUT THE POSSIBILITIES

PESSIMIST - "MY GLASS IS HALF-EMPTY"
WHAT SPARKS MY NEGATIVE SIDE?

MY CONSTRUCTIVE CRITICISM IS HELPFUL.
MY CRITICISM IS NOT!
DO I KNOW THE DIFFERENCE?

REALIST - "IT'S A GLASS OF WATER"

CLOSING THE GAP- MANAGING MY EXPECTATIONS
- FIND OUT MORE - GAIN CLARITY
- ASK OTHERS - COMMUNICATE OPENLY / CLEARLY
- ADAPT TO THE NEW - KEEP FLEXIBLE
- ENJOY THE ANTICIPATION FOR & IN ITSELF
- OFTEN IT'S THE PRE- & -POST FEELINGS THAT LAST
- UNDERSTAND YOUR REACTIONS WHEN YOUR EXPECTATIONS AREN'T MET (LEARN FROM YOURSELF)

DANGER ZONE

"I'm not in this world to live up to your expectations and you're not in this world to live up to mine."
- Bruce Lee (Martial Arts Icon, Actor, Poet, Philosopher)

MY BRAIN
LEFT VERSUS RIGHT

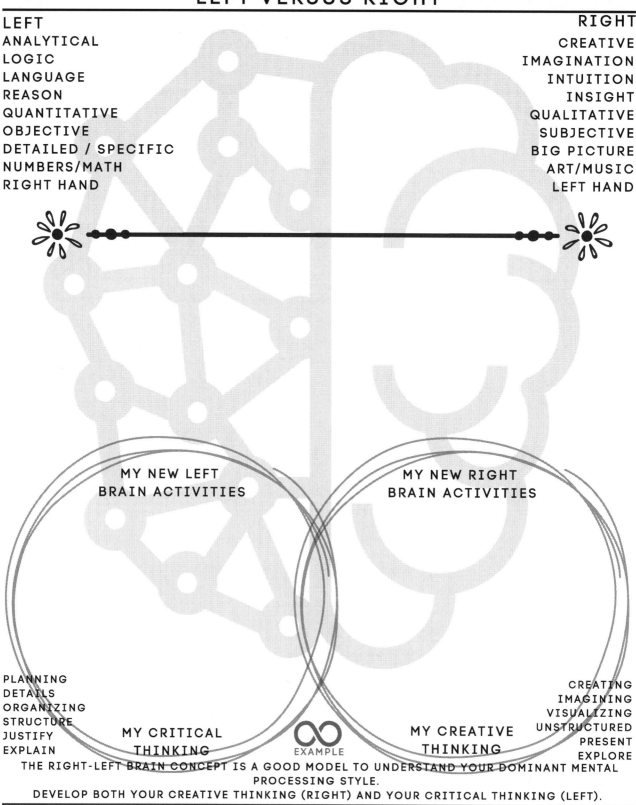

LEFT
ANALYTICAL
LOGIC
LANGUAGE
REASON
QUANTITATIVE
OBJECTIVE
DETAILED / SPECIFIC
NUMBERS/MATH
RIGHT HAND

RIGHT
CREATIVE
IMAGINATION
INTUITION
INSIGHT
QUALITATIVE
SUBJECTIVE
BIG PICTURE
ART/MUSIC
LEFT HAND

MY NEW LEFT
BRAIN ACTIVITIES

MY NEW RIGHT
BRAIN ACTIVITIES

PLANNING
DETAILS
ORGANIZING
STRUCTURE
JUSTIFY
EXPLAIN

CREATING
IMAGINING
VISUALIZING
UNSTRUCTURED
PRESENT
EXPLORE

MY CRITICAL
THINKING

EXAMPLE

MY CREATIVE
THINKING

THE RIGHT-LEFT BRAIN CONCEPT IS A GOOD MODEL TO UNDERSTAND YOUR DOMINANT MENTAL
PROCESSING STYLE.
DEVELOP BOTH YOUR CREATIVE THINKING (RIGHT) AND YOUR CRITICAL THINKING (LEFT).

"I think; therefore I am." - Rene Descartes

MY PERSPECTIVE

'PERSPECTIVE' IS YOUR MENTAL VIEW OF THE WORLD. IT'S MANIFESTED IN THE FORM OF YOUR BEHAVIOUR & YOUR ATTITUDE.
IT FORMS THE LENS IN WHICH YOU SEE LIFE AROUND YOU.

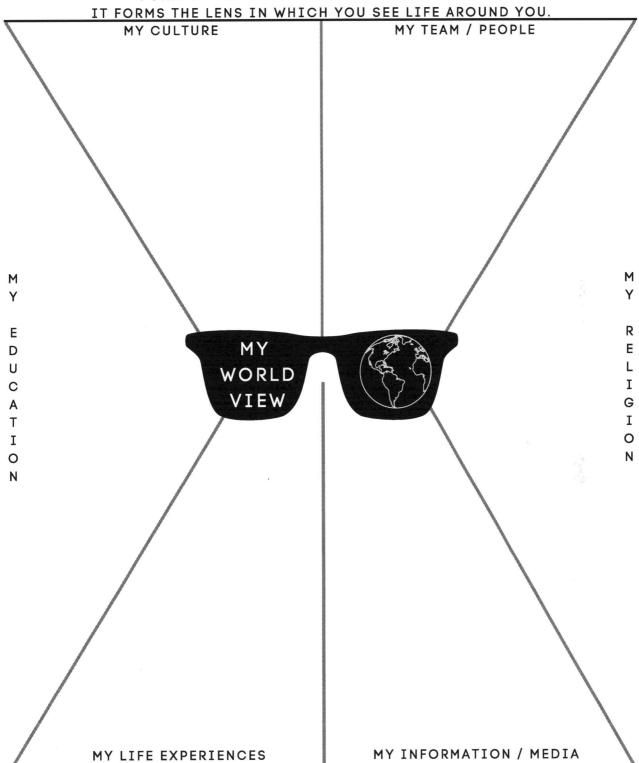

MY CULTURE

MY TEAM / PEOPLE

MY EDUCATION

MY WORLD VIEW

MY RELIGION

MY LIFE EXPERIENCES

MY INFORMATION / MEDIA

"We do not see the world we see, we see the world we can describe."
- Rene Descartes (French Philosopher, Mathematician)

MY MOTIVATIONS

YOUR MOTIVATIONS ARE PERSONAL. TYPICALLY, UNFULFILLED NEEDS ARE MORE MOTIVATING THAN FULFILLED NEEDS & FEAR IS A HUGE MOTIVATOR - BOTH POSITIVELY & NEGATIVELY; JUST MAKE SURE IT IS MOTIVATING YOU IN THE RIGHT DIRECTION!

WHAT MOTIVATES ME?

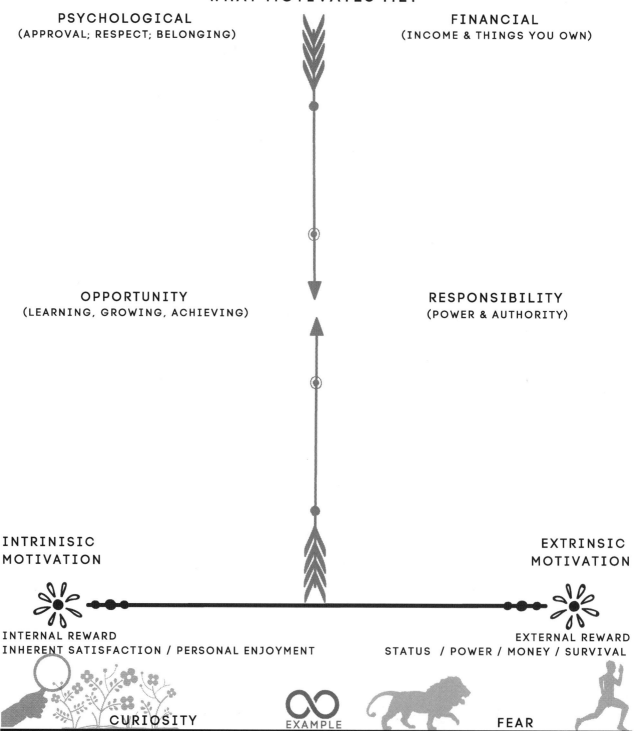

PSYCHOLOGICAL
(APPROVAL; RESPECT; BELONGING)

FINANCIAL
(INCOME & THINGS YOU OWN)

OPPORTUNITY
(LEARNING, GROWING, ACHIEVING)

RESPONSIBILITY
(POWER & AUTHORITY)

INTRINISIC
MOTIVATION

EXTRINSIC
MOTIVATION

INTERNAL REWARD
INHERENT SATISFACTION / PERSONAL ENJOYMENT

EXTERNAL REWARD
STATUS / POWER / MONEY / SURVIVAL

CURIOSITY

EXAMPLE

FEAR

"There is only one corner of the universe you can be certain of improving, and that's your own self." - Aldous Huxley (Writer)

MY DECISIONS

"DECIDE" FROM THE LATIN ROOT "DE-CAEDERE" - 'TO CUT OFF',
BY MAKING A DECISION YOU ARE CUTTING OFF OTHER ALTERNATIVES.

WHAT KIND OF DECISION?   MY DECISION
HOW IMPORTANT IS IT?

TACTICAL
(MID-LEVEL - TO MEET STRATEGIC)

OPERATIONAL
(DAILY)

STRATEGIC
(DIRECTION - LONGER TERM)

HOW URGENT IS IT?

MORE TIME TO
CONSIDER

LESS TIME TO
CONSIDER

NOT URGENT

VERY URGENT

WILL I ALIGN MY DECISION WITH MY VALUES?

TRY-TO?

NO

YES

WHAT ARE THE LONG TERM CONSEQUENCES?

I HAVE NO
IDEA

SMALL
INSIGNIFICANT

LARGE
LIFELONG

DO I HAVE OPTIONS AND ALTERNATIVES? WHAT ARE THEY?

WHEN YOU MAKE A DECISION, YOU HAVE MADE A CHOICE FROM ALTERNATIVES. ONCE
A DECISION IS MADE THEN THE NEXT STEP IS YOUR COMMITMENT TO IT,

"A good decision is based on knowledge and not numbers."
- Plato (Ancient Greek Philosopher, Writer, Teacher)

MY COMMITMENT

ANYTHING LESS THAN 100% COMMITMENT MEANS YOU ARE MORE LIKELY TO GIVE UP, RATHER THAN PUSH ON. WILLPOWER IS EASIER AT 100% COMMITMENT BECAUSE THAT IS YOUR ONLY OPTION.
YOUR DECISION IS ONLY AS STRONG AS YOUR COMMITMENT TO IT.

FOR WHATEVER TASK, GOAL, PROJECT... YOU HAVE TO DETERMINE YOUR COMMITMENT LEVEL.

WHERE ARE MY COMMITMENTS?

100% ☆
HERE, YOU HAVE CEASED LOOKING FOR ALTERNATIVES & OTHER OPTIONS

80%

WHAT IMPACTS YOUR COMMITMENT?
DIFFICULTY?
CHANCE OF SUCCESS?
CHANCE OF FAILURE?
EFFORT REQUIRED?
ALTERNATIVE OPTIONS?
TIME REQUIRED?
PRIORITIES?
YOUR ABILITY TO FULLY COMMIT?

20%

0% ∞ EXAMPLE
DECIDING TO LEARN TO FLEMENCO.
YET NOT COMMITING TO THE LEARNING PART...
THAT'S A FLAMINGO - JUST TO AVOID CONFUSION

"You may have to fight a battle more than once to win it."
- Margaret Thatcher (Former British Prime Minister)

MY FEARS

FEAR IS AN EMOTIONAL REACTION TO STIMULATION.
IT IS BOTH REAL & RATIONAL (REACTIONS FOR SURVIVAL NEEDS) &
PERCIEVED & IRRATIONAL (PERSPECTIVE OF AN EVENT / THING).
DESPITE WHAT YOU MAY THINK, YOUR FEARS ARE WITHIN YOUR INFLUENCE TO CONTROL, WELL, THE
PERCEIVED IRRATIONAL ONES ANYWAY...

ADMIT / ACCEPT

WHAT'S YOURS?

"REAL" FEAR

PERCEIVED FEAR

RECOGNIZE / IDENTIFY

SEE ALSO "MY RISKS" PG87 &
"MY WORRIES" PG67

WHERE IT COMES FROM?
CAN I IDENTIFY THE 'WHY?'

PROCESSING MY FEAR

EXPRESS MY FEELINGS?

HEALTHY DISTRACTIONS?

TALK TO SOMEONE?

HOW CAN I FACE MY FEAR?

FACE MY FEARS

"The scariest dragons and the fiercest giants usually turn out to be windmills." - Miguel de Cervantes (Spanish Writer "Don Quixote")

MY GROWTH MINDSET

FIXED MINDSET **GROWTH MINDSET**

WHOSE IN CONTROL OF MY LIFE? WHERE DO YOU IDENTIFY?

LOCUS OF CONTROL

EXTERNAL   INTERNAL

FATE CONTROLS MY FUTURE
MY FUTURE IS OUTSIDE MY CONTROL
THINGS JUST HAPPEN

I'M IN CONTROL OF MY FUTURE
I MAKE THINGS HAPPEN
OUTCOMES DETERMINED BY MY EFFORT

EFFORT

TALENT IS INBORN   TALENT THROUGH EFFORT

YOU ARE BORN WITH TALENT
EFFORT SHOWS WEAKNESS

YOU EARN TALENT
EFFORT DEVELOPS TALENT

OBSTACLES

GIVE UP   KEEP GOING

OBSTACLES STOP PROGRESS
IF IT'S TOO HARD, I GIVE UP

OBSTACLES ARE LEARNT FROM
IF IT'S TOO HARD, TRY HARDER
OR ANOTHER STRATEGY

WILLINGNESS TO LEARN

LACK CURIOSITY   ALWAYS CURIOUS

I KNOW WHAT I KNOW
I'M NOT INTERESTED TO
LEARN MORE

I HAVE SO MUCH TO LEARN
I'M ALWAYS INTERESTED TO
LEARN MORE

BIAS FOR ACTION

NO ACTION   TAKE ACTION

I WILL THINK ABOUT IT   I WILL DO IT

"Love challenges, be intrigued by mistakes, enjoy effort and never stop learning." - Carol Dweck (Creator of the Growth Mindset)

MY EFFORTS

"Knowing is not enough, we must apply. Willing is not enough. we must do." - Johann Wolfgang von Goethe (Writer, Poet, Philosopher)

WHAT DESERVES / NEEDS MY EFFORT?

ALL OTHER THINGS BEING EQUAL, WHO WILL LIKELY APPRECIATE THE VIEW FROM THE SUMMIT MORE? HIKER OR HELICOPTER?

HOW DO I VIEW OBSTACLES?

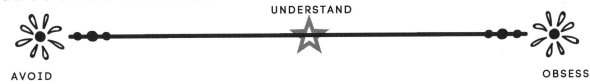

UNDERSTAND

AVOID

OBSESS

HOW DO I CELEBRATE MY SUCCESSES?   HOW AM I REWARDED FOR MY EFFORTS?
HOW DO I FEEL WHEN I ACCOMPLISH MY OBJECTIVES THROUGH EFFORT?

EFFORT & FOCUS ARE THE BIRTHPLACE OF FLOW. SEE "MY FLOW" PG 74.

"Even though it was so difficult, there was not another thing in the world I would rather have been doing." - Terry Fox
AFTER A BATTLE WITH CANCER, CAUSING HIS LEG TO BE AMPUTATED. TERRY STARTED HIS "MARATHON OF HOPE" - RUNNING ACROSS CANADA & RAISING MONEY FOR CANCER RESEARCH. HIS COURAGEOUS STORY & DETERMINED EFFORT CONTINUES TO INSPIRE HOPE & RAISE MILLIONS.

"The most difficult thing is the decision to act,
the rest is merely tenacity.
The fears are the paper tigers.
You can do anything you decide to do.
You can act to change and control your life,
and the procedure,
the process is its own reward"

- Amelia Earhart

PIONEER ADVENTURER & FIRST FEMALE TO FLY THE ATLANTIC SOLO

MY GRIT

"Grit is passion & sustained persistence applied toward long-term achievement. It combines resilience, ambition & self-control in the pursuit of goals that take months, years, or even decades."
- Angela Duckworth (Psychology Researcher, Professor)

GUTS   WHAT DO I WANT? DO I HAVE THE COURAGE?

G

"GUTS" = PERSONAL COURAGE & DETERMINATION; GUT FEELING; & 'THE GUT' IN YOUR STOMACH. ITS MENTIONED A LOT HERE!

RESILIENCE   MY BARRIERS & OBSTACLES TO OVERCOME

R

WHETHER METAPHORICALLY OR PHYSICALLY LOOKING AFTER YOUR GUT MAY WELL DO WONDERS IN YOUR LIFE!

RESILIENCY - SOMETHING WE ALL NEED

INITIATIVE   DISCOVERING NEW WAYS TO MEET MY CHALLENGES

I

TENACITY   WHY? HOW WILL THIS HELP? MY DETERMINATION TO CONTINUE

T

"I attribute my success to this; I never gave or took an excuse." - Florence Nightingale ('Founder' of Modern Nursing)

MY RESILIENCY

"The art of victory is learned in defeat."
- Simon Bolivar ('El Libertador' to many Latin Americans)

WHAT IS MY DEFAULT REACTION TO MISTAKES / FAILURE?

- GIVE UP
- KEEP GOING
- CRY - SULK
- BLAME OTHERS
- MAKE EXCUSES
- LEARN FROM IT
- BLOCK IT OUT
- DISTRACTION

SEE " MY MOMENTS OF WEAKNESS" PG 61

HOW CAN I LEARN TO DEVELOP MY REACTIONS TO LOSS?

"SILVER LININGS"

THE POSITIVE THINGS THAT COME FROM NEGATIVE EVENTS. COINED BY JOHN MILTON (17TH CENTURY)

"TO LAUGH AT YOURSELF IS TO LOVE YOURSELF".

AS MICKEY MOUSE SAID. WE ALL DO STUPID THINGS AT TIMES; PUT IT IN CONTEXT, STAY HUMBLE & DON'T TAKE YOURSELF TOO SERIOUSLY...

- FOCUS ON THE BIG PICTURE (YOU CAN'T WIN EVERY TIME)
- IS MY REACTION HARMFUL OR HELPFUL? (WHAT ARE THE REAL CONSEQUENCES?)
- WHAT HAVE I LEARNT? (THAT CAN TAKE SOME TIME...)
- WHAT IS A NEW STATEGY? (CAN I CHANGE COURSE?)
- DO I HAVE THE COURAGE TO ADMIT MY OWN MISTAKES?
- WHAT IS THE "SILVER LINING"?

HOW CAN I PRACTICE HUMILITY?

HUMILITY IS A STRENGTH, IT MEANS;
- YOU ARE NOT ALWAYS RIGHT
- YOU DON'T HAVE ALL THE ANSWERS
- YOU GENUINELY LISTEN TO OTHERS
- YOU ASK FOR HELP IF YOU NEED IT
- YOU ARE ALWAYS LEARNING
- YOU SHOW APPRECIATION
- YOU ARE HUMAN & MAKE MISTAKES & THAT'S OKAY!

HUMILITY DOES NOT MEAN A LACK OF SELF-CONFIDENCE, IT MEANS THAT YOU ARE WILLING TO LISTEN.

"Be like bamboo; the higher you grow, the deeper the bow."
- Chinese Proverb

MY CONFIDENCE

CONFIDENCE COMES FROM THE LATIN WORD "FIDERE" = "TO TRUST".
THEREFORE, SELF-CONFIDENCE IS TO "TRUST YOURSELF"

WHEN DO I FEEL MOST STRONG? SHOW TRUST IN MYSELF.

MANTRAS FOR MY SUCCESS - WORDS THAT EMPOWER & INSPIRE

MANTRAS
ARE OVER 3500 YEARS OLD
SANSKRIT LANGUAGE ROOT
"MANAS" - MIND
"TRA" - TOOL
SO MANTRAS ARE MIND TOOLS.
THEY ARE SOUNDS, WORDS &
PHRASES
WHICH ARE REPEATED &
USED TO INSPIRE, CALM
& FOCUS THE MIND

"FAKE IT 'TIL YOU MAKE IT." - HOW CAN I SHOW CONFIDENCE?

OWN IT!
WHEN YOU OWN IT,
YOU DON'T ALLOW ANYONE
TO BRING YOU DOWN!
YOU TAKE RESPONSIBILITY
FOR YOUR ACTIONS,
CHOICES & MISTAKES
YOU WILL EARN RESPECT,
DEVELOP SELF-ESTEEM &
GROW IN
CONFIDENCE.

OWNING IT
INSTEAD OF MAKING EXCUSES, YOU ARE ABLE TO LEARN
& DEVELOP YOUR SKILLS, GAINING CONFIDENCE.

"Inaction breeds doubt and fear. Action breeds confidence and courage. If you want to conquer fear, do not sit at home and think about it. Go out and get busy." - Dale Carnegie (Author)

MY OPENNESS TO CHANGE
WHEN FORCES COLLIDE

WHATS PUSHING ME TO CHANGE?

WHAT'S MOTIVIATING, DRIVING THE
CHANGE? WHY CHANGE?

WHATS KEEPING ME THE SAME?

WHAT'S MAINTAINING THE STATUS-QUO?
WHY STAY THE SAME?

CHANGE FORCE

STAY THE SAME FORCE

YIN & YANG

"TAIJITU" -
'DARK - BRIGHT'
IS THE TAOIST CHINESE PHILOSOPHY
OF DUALISM, POSITIVE / NEGATIVE,
MALE / FEMALE - BUT RARELY IS IT
SIMPLY BLACK & WHITE

"TAEGEUK"
THE TRADITIONAL KOREAN SYMBOL
OF 'THE SUPREME ULTIMATE'.
SEEN ON THE SOUTH KOREAN FLAG.
IT REPRESENTS BALANCE IN THE
UNIVERSE, RED & BLUE -
DUALISM & HARMONY.

BASED ON THE FORCE-FIELD ANALYSIS BY KURT LEWIN, 'FOUNDER' OF SOCIAL PSYCHOLOGY

"It is not the strongest or the most intelligent who will survive, but
those who can best manage change"
- Charles Darwin (Biologist, Naturalist, Explorer, Pioneer)

MY SUCCESS

"The biggest adventure you can ever take is to live the life of your Dreams" - Oprah Winfrey (Living her Dream)

WHAT DOES SUCCESS MEAN TO ME?

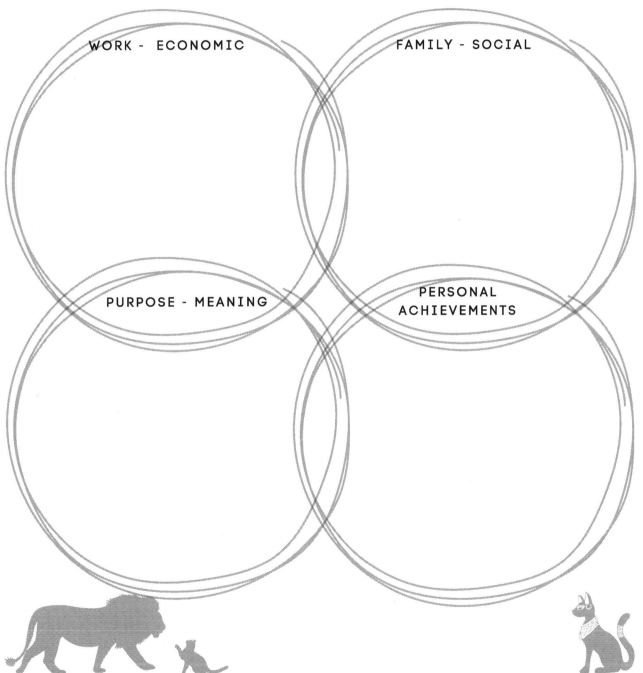

WORK - ECONOMIC

FAMILY - SOCIAL

PURPOSE - MEANING

PERSONAL ACHIEVEMENTS

PERHAPS THE MOST SUCCESSFUL OF MAMMALS ISN'T YOU HUMANS AFTER ALL - THAT MAY BELONG TO THE 'FILIDAE' - THE FELINE. NOT ONLY DO 'CATS' RULE YOUR HUMAN HOMES; THEY RULE THE JUNGLE, AS THEY HAVE CONQUERED ALL LANDSCAPES & CLIMATES. FROM THE AFRICAN PLAINS TO THE ARCTIC TUNDRA, THEY HAVE EVEN BEEN WORSHIPPED AS GODS, NOT BAD FOR A KITTY-CAT.

SPIRITUAL / ALTRUISTIC

MY GOALS / OUTCOMES

"This is my simple religion. There is no need for temples; no need for complicated philosophy. Our own brain, our own heart is our temple; the philosophy is kindness."
- 14th Dalai Lama

SPIRITUAL / ALTRUISTIC

Your Spiritual World is the 8th and final world. This world is the one many humans find polarizing, being the most or least comfortable in. This is mostly due to the mystery, the power and the unknown that this world is known for. The 7th and highest of the 7 chakras, this energy center sits above the head, it's the energy you release into the world. It's the world that sits outside yourself, that's because it's bigger than yourself! It encompasses both your search for meaning but also where you feel a profound sense of belonging.

Your Spiritual World does not need to be a religious one, although it can be.
'Spiritual' is a word that has many perspectives. In this case it means simply, 'higher than yourself' or, 'greater than yourself'. For some people this will come to mean God or religion as their principal belief system and connection with the divine. But this is just one of many spiritual paths and journeys.

'Altruism' is the other term to describe this world, if you prefer? Altruism is when you have a genuine concern for the wellbeing of others, not just human life, but all life.

Being Altruistic means that you look outside yourself for the greater good of the people or places around you. You put your life in the service of others, it's not all about you. The starting point, if you need one, is; 'To Look Beyond Yourself'.

SPIRITUAL

"HIGHER THAN YOURSELF"

"GREATER THAN YOURSELF"

Based on my extensive research, across history, religion and philosophy. Altruism, sits in the 7th chakra as it's giving, helping others and it's outside of you. I have noticed, it's a concept across all your religions, every single one, they're all about being 'Altruistic'. That's why these terms go hand-in-hand. Personally, as your workbook, I'm most satisfied when I'm helping you, my companion on this journey. What about you?

ALTRUISM

LATIN WORD "ALTERI" "SOMEONE ELSE" OR "OTHER".

For some, spirituality is the unknown, a complex force of energy, for others, it lies in nature. You may disagree, but science itself is a form of spirituality, looking for deeper answers and meaning to the fundamental questions on life. Physicists, Biologists and Astronomers looking at the creation of the universe, The Big-Bang. This is also a belief system, there may be equations but they are still theories, it's whether you believe in them that matters. Even though there are images and flight paths to "prove" a spherical planet Earth, there are still those who believe, or want to believe, it's flat.

This is also a world in which meditation, reflection and prayer can play an important role. Allowing yourself times of quiet solitude to reflect, find inner-harmony, pray to the divine, or meditate for a deeper connection or focus within.

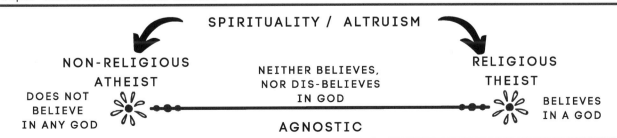

SPIRITUALITY / ALTRUISM

NON-RELIGIOUS
ATHEIST

NEITHER BELIEVES,
NOR DIS-BELIEVES
IN GOD

RELIGIOUS
THEIST

DOES NOT
BELIEVE
IN ANY GOD

BELIEVES
IN A GOD

AGNOSTIC

SPIRITUAL / ALTRUISTIC

Humans are very good at spotting patterns, recognizing sequences and observing repeated events. Our memories and communication tools have helped us better understand the patterns of stars, planets, seasons, weather, days, tides and our own bodies. As a species, we're constantly searching for more, looking for meaning and searching for greater understanding.

Stories are the fabric of human cultures. Storytelling is how knowledge was passed on throughout generations, the humble story has had a large impact on all global civilizations. First verbally, and then through written text and scriptures. TV shows and movies have taken over storytelling more recently.

**STORY
=
HISTORIA
(HISTORY)**

Stories are based on both real events and fictional ones. History is the telling of the real stories of the past. The word 'Story' is derived from 'History', but as many historians will attest, that too is written from someone's perspective and recollection of events.

Some stories are very special and have great meaning and significance for billions of people all over the planet. The scriptures and holy books guide behaviour and can offer wisdom and inspiration to the many who have faith in their word.

Faith is an important part of this world. Faith in God or in a Higher Power is an important tenant in most religions. Faith is simply defined as "your confidence" in something. If you have faith in it, it means you have confidence in it. Your faith in this world is the confidence you have in your belief system. Your spirituality is deeply personal, as is your faith.

**"FAITH"
=
YOUR
CONFIDENCE IN
SOMETHING**

For most of the Indigenous populations around the world, which grew and developed independently of each other, oral stories were the way values, beliefs and cultural traditions were passed on. Indigenous people connect their spirituality with their land and environment, nature is revered and respected. Much like in western thought with the concept of "Mother Nature", the environment has been personified so all humans could somehow explain her many magical faces. Can you imagine how you would feel and explain the magic of a rainbow? Or the terror of a thunderstorm, 2000 years ago?

A deep part of the many paths of spirituality is the connection with both the environment, as well as ancestor's past. Many cultures show great reverence and care for their ancestors and guard and pass on their hi-stories. Teachers of the past also act as guides and spirituality is a feeling of connectedness and community.

For whatever this world is for you, if you want to give life greater meaning and purpose, then you need to cultivate something "Greater than Yourself". Be that through; your faith in God, belief in Science, search for Nirvana, or simply through your sense of Service to Others. Here your Greatness goes beyond yourself.

In this world and throughout our journey together, you have the chance of creating your own mission or philosophy to live by. Your own thoughtful values governing your life, to live it the best way you can. One that is based on what's most important to you and those closest to you. Here's a chance to create your own Spiritual World and completely change your Whole World.

MY MEANING & PURPOSE

WHAT GIVES ME PURPOSE?

WHAT GIVES ME GUIDANCE?

MY TIME TO
REFLECT / PRAY / MEDITATE

CREATING AWE (SOME)

HEAVEN
SNOWFLAKES DROP FROM THE HEAVENS IN A MAGICAL ARRAY OF GEOMETRICAL SHAPES - CREATING BEAUTY, PROVIDING NOURISHMENT & GIVING LIFE.

SNOW REPRESENTS PURITY. IT'S A SYMBOL OF CHRISTMAS FOR SOME & OF WINTER FOR OTHERS. IT'S A WATER SOURCE & PLEASURE GIVER TO BILLIONS.

EARTH

"Burn worldly love, rub the ashes and make the ink of it, make the heart the pen, the intellect the writer, write that which has no end or limit." - Guru Nanak Dev Ji (1st Guru - Founder of Sikhism)

MY HOPE

HOPE IS YOUR GREATEST ALLY WHEN TIMES ARE TOUGH. MAINTAINING HOPE & FINDING WAYS TO BE HOPEFUL BUILDS RESILIENCE, AS YOU LOOK TOWARDS A POSITIVE FUTURE.

"I dwell in Possibility." - Emily Dickinson

H

WHAT GIVES ME HOPE?

O

OPPORTUNITIES TO BE HOPEFUL

P

PEOPLE WHO INSPIRE HOPE

E

EXPERIENCES I AM HOPEFUL FOR

"Turn and face the sun and let your shadow fall behind you."
- Maori Proverb

MY INTEGRITY

MY LIFE
VALUES

THE STATE
OF BEING
COMPLETE
WHOLE

ADHERENCE
TO A CODE
(YOUR CODE OF
CONDUCT)

HOW MY
ACTIONS
ALIGN WITH
THESE VALUES?

1

2

3

4

5

6

7

8

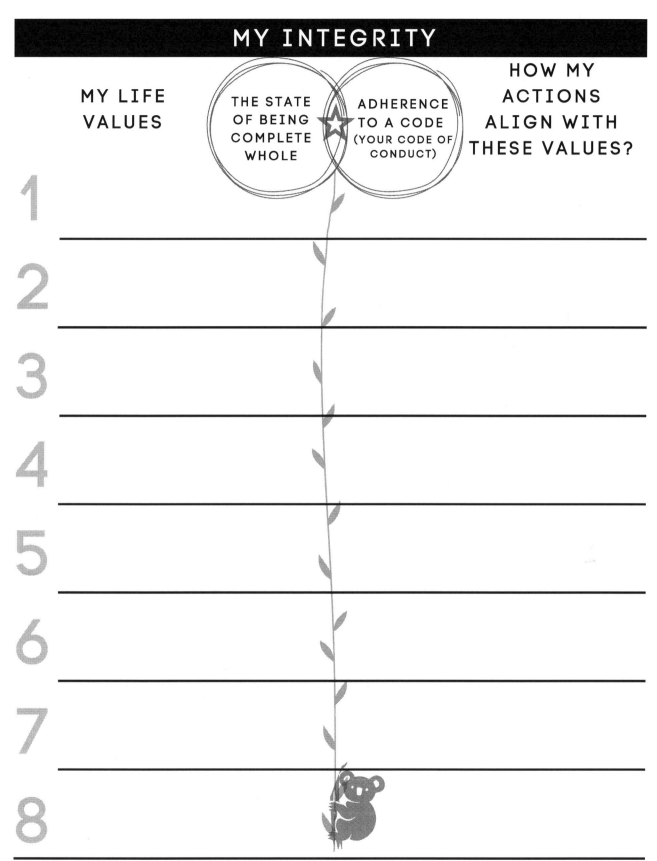

THE OPPOSITE = HYPOCRISY (FROM GREEK - "ACTING A THEATRICAL PART" - "PRETEND" - BEING
HYPOCRITCAL MEANS SAYING ONE THING, YET ACTING IN ANOTHER WAY. ACTING WITH INTEGRITY
MEANS YOUR WORDS ALIGN WITH YOUR ACTIONS, WHICH ALIGN WITH YOUR VALUES.

"AUTHENTIC" = 'REAL' OR 'GENUINE'
"REAL" = NOT FAKE OR IMPERSONATED

AM I LIVING MY REAL - AUTHENTIC LIFE?

"Remembering that I'll be dead soon is the most important tool I've ever encountered to help me make the big choices in life.
Because almost everything - all external expectations,
all pride, all fear of embarrassment or failure -
these things just fall away in the face of death,
leaving only what is truly important.
Remembering that you are going to die is the best way i know to avoid the trap of thinking you have something to lose.
You are already naked.
There is no reason not to follow your heart."
- Steve Jobs (Visionary Founder of Apple Inc.)

WHAT DO I WANT TO CREATE?

HOW DO I WANT TO BE REMEMBERED?

"It is not God's will merely that we should be happy, but that we should make ourselves happy."
- Immanuel Kant (German Philosopher, Enlightenment Thinker)

MY FIVE ELEMENTS
BALANCING MY ELEMENTS FROM THE EAST

LIVING PASSIONATELY
LIVING WITH INTENSITY

PROMOTING
GROWTH
STRENGTHEN MY
CURIOSITY

LIVING
HONESTLY
LIVING WITH
INTEGRITY

FIRE

火

木
WOOD

五行

土
EARTH

水
WATER

金
METAL

LIVING WITH STILLNESS & CALM
PRACTICALITY & RESOURCEFULNESS

THINKING RATIONALITY
& LOGICALLY

WU-XING IS A CHINESE-BASED PHILOSOPHY OF 5 ELEMENTS / CHI / ENERGY /
SYSTEMS & THE ACTIONS & INTERACTIONS OF THESE. ONCE AGAIN, SEEKING
BALANCE & HARMONY OF THESE 5 INTERCONNECTING WORLDS.

MY SUSTAINABILITY
THE THREE PILLARS OF SUSTAINABILITY

SUSTAINABILITY IS 'TO SUSTAIN' = TO MAINTAIN, NOT DEGRADE.
IT'S A LONG-TERM OUTLOOK; INSTEAD OF JUST CONSIDERING THE SHORT-TERM
GAIN. IT COMES BACK TO THE WORD; 'BALANCE' SUSTAINABILITY IS BALANCE.

WHAT AM I DOING TO SUSTAIN THE PLANET & LIFE ITSELF?
CHANGES I CAN MAKE LOCALLY TO CONTRIBUTE GLOBALLY

ENVIRONMENTAL

SOCIAL / CULTURAL

WHAT AM I DOING TO SUSTAIN RELATIONSHIPS & FRIENDSHIPS?
HOW AM I MAINTAINING MY CULTURAL HERITAGE / KNOWLEDGE?
HOW CAN I STAY CURIOUS & KEEP LEARNING ABOUT OTHERS?

ECONOMIC

WHAT AM I DOING TO SUSTAIN MY FINANCIAL SITUATION?
HOW AM I STAYING RELEVANT? UPSKILL?
HOW CAN I CONTINUE TO STAY PASSIONATE?

"Each one of us matters, has a role to play, and makes a difference.
Each one of us must take responsibility for our own lives, and above
all, show respect and love for living things around us, especially each
other." - Jane Goodall (Primatologist, Anthropologist)

MY FREEDOM

"The most courageous act is still to think for yourself. Aloud."
- Coco Chanel (Fashion Icon - Free Spirit)

AM I FREE TO CHOOSE?
DO I FEEL I HAVE CHOICE?

"-DOM" - OLD ENGLISH MEANING 'JUDGEMENT', STATE, CONDITION.

"FREE" - NOT UNDER THE CONTROL OF ANOTHER POWER.

'FREE' +' DOM' = 'YOUR JUDGEMENT OF YOUR SELF-DETERMINATION'

YOUR FREEDOM GIVES YOU A RIGHT TO CHOOSE.
A CHOICE IN HOW YOU LIVE YOUR LIFE.

AM I FREE TO BELIEVE?

AM I FREE TO INVESTIGATE / EXPLORE THE TRUTH?

AM I FREE TO BE MYSELF?

AM I FREE TO EXPRESS MYSELF IN HEALTHY WAYS?

GET RESPECT

GIVE RESPECT

CREATE MORE FREEDOM BY;
- TAKING CONTROL OF THE THINGS YOU HAVE CONTROL OVER.
- UNDERSTANDING & REACTING YOUR BEST TO THE AREAS YOU CAN'T CONTROL.
- STAYING CURIOUS - ASKING QUESTIONS, EXPLORING ANSWERS.
- FOLLOWING YOUR OWN PATH & YOUR OWN VALUES.
- FREEDOM IS A JUDGEMENT - WHAT CAN YOU DO ABOUT IT?
- IF YOU EXPECT FREEDOM - YOU NEED TO RESPECT THE FREEDOM OF OTHERS!
- RESPECT IS TWO WAY - YOU CAN'T EXPECT RESPECT IF YOU DON'T GIVE IT.

"No one outside ourselves can rule us inwardly. When we know this, we become free." - Gautama Buddha

MY CONTENTMENT

CONTENTMENT = STATE OF SATISFACTION & PEACE

WHEN DO I FEEL MOST AT EASE / SATISFIED ?

'CONTENT' COMES FROM LATIN "CONTENTUS"

SATISFIED + STRETCHED, STRAINED

CONTENT DOESN'T MEAN 'DOING NOTHING' IT MEANS BEING SATISFIED WITH WHAT YOU ARE DOING!

WHOSE COMPANY DO I FEEL MOST CONTENT?

WHAT BRINGS ME SATISFACTION/PEACE, JUST THINKING ABOUT IT?

HOW CAN I CREATE OPPORTUNITES FOR INNER- PEACE?

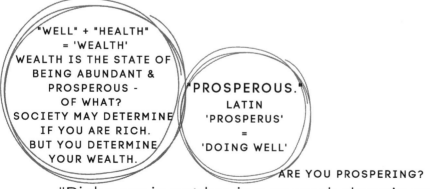

"WELL" + "HEALTH" = 'WEALTH' WEALTH IS THE STATE OF BEING ABUNDANT & PROSPEROUS - OF WHAT? SOCIETY MAY DETERMINE IF YOU ARE RICH. BUT YOU DETERMINE YOUR WEALTH.

'PROSPEROUS.' LATIN 'PROSPERUS' = 'DOING WELL'

ARE YOU PROSPERING?

"Richness is not having many belongings, but richness is contentment of the soul."- Prophet Muhammad- Peace Be Upon Him

"The most important kind of freedom
is to be what you really are.
You trade in your reality for a role.
Your trade in your sense for an act.
You give up our ability to feel,
and in exchange, put on a mask.
There can't be any large-scale
revolution until there's a personal
revolution,
on an individual level.
It's got to happen inside first."

- Jim Morrison

MY INSPIRATION

MY TIME TO MEDITATE / PRAY / REFLECT / CREATE / CONNECT

CREATE TIME TO MAKE POSITIVE HABITS

MY PLACE

MY TIME

MY FREQUENCY

BENEFITS OF MEDITATION
- INCREASED FOCUS
- PROMOTES EMOTIONAL HEALTH
- REDUCES STRESS
- CONTROLS ANXIETY
- REDUCES INFLAMMATION
- INCREASES COGNITION - CREATIVITY & NEW IDEAS
- CREATES SENSE OF CALM / PEACE / BALANCE

WHY I MEDITATE?

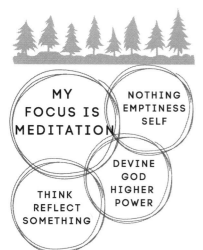

MY FOCUS IS MEDITATION

NOTHING EMPTINESS SELF

DEVINE GOD HIGHER POWER

THINK REFLECT SOMETHING

WHAT STOPPING ME FROM MAKING THE TIME?

SOLUTIONS
START SMALL
HAVE A TIME
HAVE A PLACE
NO INTERRUPTIONS
ADD A REMINDER
GET COMFORTABLE
NO EXPECTATIONS -
JUST SIT WITH YOURSELF

MEDITATION IS OFTEN CONSIDERED RELIGIOUS, & IT CAN BE.
"TO MEDITATE" IS DERIVED FROM THE LATIN "MEDITATIO" - 'TO THINK OR REFLECT UPON.'
MEDITATION IS YOUR FOCUS ON EITHER SOMETHING SPECIFIC, NOTHING, OR THE DEVINE.

"Our mind is enriched by what we receive, our heart by what we give."
- Victor Hugo (French Novelist, Poet, National Hero)

MY GRATITUDE & GRATEFULNESS

GRATITUDE IS A PROFOUND & SINCERE RESPECT. IT MEANS YOU APPRECIATE LIFE ITSELF, THE PEOPLE IN IT & ITS MANY MYSTERIES. IT MEANS NOT TAKING LIFE 'FOR GRANTED' & SAYING THANK-YOU FOR ALL THAT IT HAS TAKEN TO GET YOU HERE. TO THIS VERY MOMENT. YES, NOW!

THE PEOPLE IN MY LIFE

THE PLACES IN MY LIFE

THE EXPERIENCES I HAVE HAD

THE PLANET & LIFE ITSELF

"Give thanks for a little & receive a lot."
- Hansa Proverb

"Gratitude turns what we have into enough."
- Aesop (Ancient Greek storyteller ~600BC)

MY GIVING BACK

"No one has ever become poor by giving." - Anne Frank

SOCIAL - HELP OTHERS	EDUCATIONAL - LEARN
ENVIRONMENTAL - HELP THE PLANET	ECONOMIC - DONATE TIME & RESOURCES

"Everyone has the power for GREATness - not for fame but greatness, because greatness is determined by service."
- Martin Luther King Jr. (US Civil Rights Leader)

MY JUDGEMENT

IN THE END OF THE DAY, ON PLANET EARTH, YOU ARE YOUR OWN JUDGE.
ONLY YOU DECIDE IF YOU'RE LIVING THE LIFE YOU WANT,
ONE THAT REFLECTS WHO YOU REALLY ARE; ONLY YOU CAN KNOW.
YOU'LL LISTEN TO THE JUDGEMENTS FROM OTHERS,
BUT FOR YOUR OWN WELL-BEING, IT'S YOUR OWN JUDGEMENT OF YOURSELF
THAT ACTUALLY MATTERS.

HOW CAN I BE A BETTER, MORE
POSITIVE JUDGE OF MYSELF?

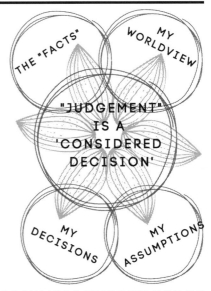

THE "FACTS"

MY WORLDVIEW

"JUDGEMENT"
IS A
'CONSIDERED
DECISION'

MY DECISIONS

MY ASSUMPTIONS

HOW MUCH DO I ASSUME? WITHOUT PROOF

ASSUMPTION = A JUDGEMENT WITHOUT PROOF

HOW CAN I USE BETTER JUDGEMENT? BE A FAIRER JUDGE OF OTHERS?

YES, I CHOSE TO SPELL JUDGEMENT WITH AN "E"

THE WORD
"JUDGEMENT"
IS GIVEN A BAD NAME.
ALL ANIMALS, INCLUDING
HUMANS, MAKE JUDGEMENTS,
FOR SURVIVAL &
TO MAKE DECISIONS.
SO INSTEAD OF TRYING NOT TO
JUDGE.
TRY TO BE A MORE ACCURATE
& COMPASSIONATE JUDGE;
OF YOURSELF
& OTHERS.

"Someone will always be prettier. Someone will be smarter.
Someone will always be younger. But they will never be you."
- Freddie Mercury (Music Icon & Breaker of Barriers)

THE GOLDEN SPIRAL

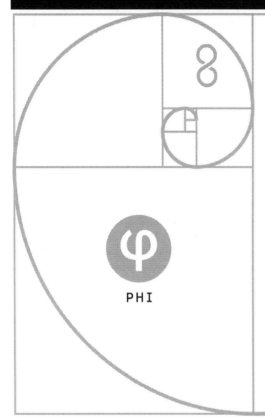

THE GOLDEN SPIRAL IS BASED ON THE GOLDEN RATIO, OR THE FIBONACCI SEQUENCE.
STUDIED BY THE ANCIENT GREEKS & MATHEMATICIANS THROUGHOUT THE MIDDLE EAST & ASIA.
IT WAS POPULARIZED BY MATHEMATICIAN - LEONARDO OF PISA, A GREAT MIND OF THE MIDDLE AGES, KNOWN AS "FIBONACCI".
CAN YOU FIGURE OUT THE PATTERN?

PHI

FIBONACCI SEQUENCE

0 , 1 , 1 , 2 , 3 , 5 , 8 , 13 , 21 , 34 , 55 , 89 , 144 , 233

The 'divine proportion' is seen throughout nature.
From the way sea shells create their shells;
to the the way a fern unfurls its fronds.
It's a symbol of new beginnings for some cultures;
while signifies the mystic & the unknown in others.
It guides our galaxies & the way planets move;
to how petals grow on flowers & leaves on trees.
The Golden Spiral brings together the magic & mystery of
nature with the insight & ingenuity of mathematics in a
beautiful fusion.
Human knowledge & Natural wonder.

"Science cannot solve the ultimate mystery of nature. And that is because, in the last analysis, we ourselves are part of the mystery that we are trying to solve." - Max Planck (Nobel Winning Physicist)

MY CURIOSITY LIST

WHY CAN'T POLAR BEARS EAT PENGUINS?

"I have no special talents, I am only passionately curious."
- Albert Einstein (Curious Soul, Explorer of "Why?")

MY 16 HOURS
WHERE ARE YOUR 16 HOURS TAKING YOU?

"Do you think that I count the days?
There is only one day left,
always starting over:
it is given to us at dawn
and taken away from us at dusk."

- Jean-Paul Sartre

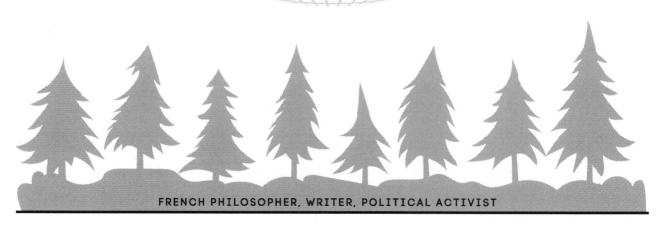

FRENCH PHILOSOPHER, WRITER, POLITICAL ACTIVIST

MY **GREAT** LIFE

BRINGING MY WORLDS TO LIFE

MY LIFE VALUES

MY LIFE MISSION

MY LIFE 8

MY 16 HOURS

SPIRITUAL / ALTRUISTIC
GIVING TIME

MENTAL
GROWTH TIME

SOCIAL
SHARING TIME

INTIMATE
INTIMATE TIME

TECHNOLOGICAL
ME TIME

WORK / CREATIVE
CREATIVE TIME

PHYSICAL
MOVEMENT TIME

ENVIRONMENTAL
APPRECIATION TIME

LEONARDO DA VINCI'S VITRUVIAN MAN

Giving Time
Time to Help Others, Give Back, Reflect, Prayer, Meditate

Growth Time
Time to Focus & Learn

Me Time
Time for Yourself

Sharing Time
Time to Share with Others

Intimate Time
Time for Trust & Emotional Connection

Creation Time
Time to Build, Make, Create

Movement Time
Time to Move your Body

MY ∞ TIMES

Appreciation Time
Time for Appreciating & Connecting with your Environment / Place

MY 16 HOURS

As you journey through your 8 Worlds, you'll discover more about who you are.
My goal as your companion on this journey is two-fold; the first is creating awareness, greater awareness of your current lifestyle choices, behaviours and challenges.
While secondly, it is to encourage and support you on action-based solutions.

I love spending time with you but you also need to be smart about your own time. When you think about it, all you have is the time you have. None of us know how long or short that time will be. Look at me, one slip into a bathtub and I'm history!

That's why the next stage on your journey is to bring your 8 Worlds into your Real World. And how do you do that? Your World Time Zones. The 24 hour day, in reality, is 16 hours for most (once we take away 8 for sleep). Your 16 hours everyday matter. Your time is valuable, but do you value your time? Use your World Time Zones as a way to see more value in the hours you have, everyday.

In the final section, you will explore a framework and tools designed to spark action and turn your enhanced awareness into Your Time. You don't need to have completed all pages before looking into this chapter, but if you haven't read it yet;

'KNOWLEDGE ALONE CHANGES LITTLE
UNLESS IT'S ACTED UPON.'
&
'YOUR KNOWLEDGE BECOMES YOUR
WISDOM ONCE IT'S ACTED UPON & IN
YOUR OWN EXPERIENCE.'

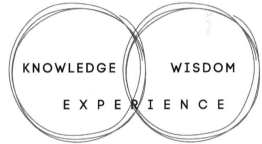

TO TURN YOUR KNOWLEDGE INTO YOUR WISDOM, YOU NEED TIME!

If you don't include it in your schedule, it won't be done, so that's why Worlds turn into Time. Your 8 World's parallel into 8 Time-Zones. These are zones where you fulfil certain actions to meet the needs in each of your worlds.

GIVING TIME
TIME FOR HELPING OTHERS, GIVING
GROWTH TIME
TIME TO CONCENTRATE, LEARNING
SHARING TIME
TIME TO BE SOCIAL
INTIMATE TIME
TIME TO YOUR TRUSTED CONNECTIONS
CREATION TIME
TIME TO MAKE, BUILD, CREATE
MOVEMENT TIME
TIME TO MOVE YOUR BODY.
APPRECITATION TIME
TIME TO BE THANKFUL & RESPECT OF PLACE
ME TIME
TIME TO ENJOY WHAT YOU LOVE

By making time for each area and bringing them into the conscious, you're being purposeful. Purpose creates fulfilment. By creating time for each area you'll also find more balance.

Each of these times correlate to your 8 Worlds and your daily wellbeing. They are NOT mutually exclusive, you can combine Times. In fact, they should be combined.

Here, you will see how you can incorporate all these important facets into your daily routine for a fuller, more purposeful life.

MY 16 HOURS

The main reason I created this section was due to the many excuses humans use around the concept of 'Time', namely, "Not having enough of it!" It's certainly one of the most frequent excuses I see written on my pages. But this excuse has many holes in it (little circles again). You have the time, you just need to find ways to best use it.

Let's look at an example, cooking dinner, this can be a chore and a bore. But if you think of it as an occasion to bring your family/friends together (Sharing Time), try cooking something new (Growth Time), or teach someone the recipe (Giving Time), put on some music and dance (safely) (Movement Time). Create a dish with local ingredients/recipe, share the story and enjoy. (Appreciation Time)

Let's try another one, study. The most important thing is what that study is for, it's propelling you forward in positive ways, remember the 'Why'. That maintains the motivation. Study can give you 'Me time'. Your main goal here is focus and learning, so that is 'Growth Time'. Mix it up by adding in a study buddy and you'll have 'Share Time'. Include 'Movement Time' as a reward for your efforts and stretch your muscles.

I have noticed another side-effect when you mix up your world time zones; Creativity. Combining your worlds in new ways will not just save you time and help you feel more fulfilled; it'll also spark creative solutions, ways and methods. Creativity sparks when you combine things in new and interesting ways. By being conscious of your World Time Zones, you're ensuring you are making the most of your 16 Hours.

Mixing it up, changing things around can be annoying and fear inducing, but by changing things up, you keep life interesting and importantly; lessen your Hedonic Adaptation (the kind you don't want).

Hedonic Adaptation or (Treadmill) is the human quality to adapt back to a baseline of 'happiness', after either, positive or negative events. This can be seen as both good and bad. Basically, humans 'get used to stuff'. After a while, most people don't get the same pleasure (or pain) from the 'new' stimulus or event.

A Ferrari is just a car after you drive it for a while and losing your job may seem like the end of the world, but remarkably, you'll recover. Time may not heal all wounds completely, but it helps the process of moving on, bouncing back and looking forward.

Philosophers and religious leaders have all spoken of this concept. Scientists have confirmed it. To stop boredom, mix it up. Have a routine, but then change it. Use your Times creatively and find new ways to combine your worlds to keep them interesting.

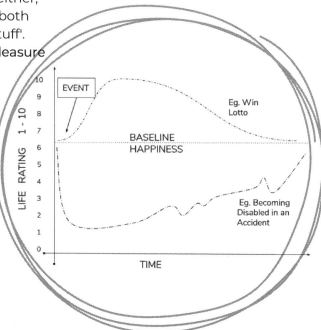

HEDONIC ADAPTATION

BRAINSTORM - TIME ZONES

INTER-LOCKING CIRCLES REPRESENT THE MANY VARIED & INTERCONNECTED WAYS TO COMBINE YOUR WORLDS. GET CREATING!

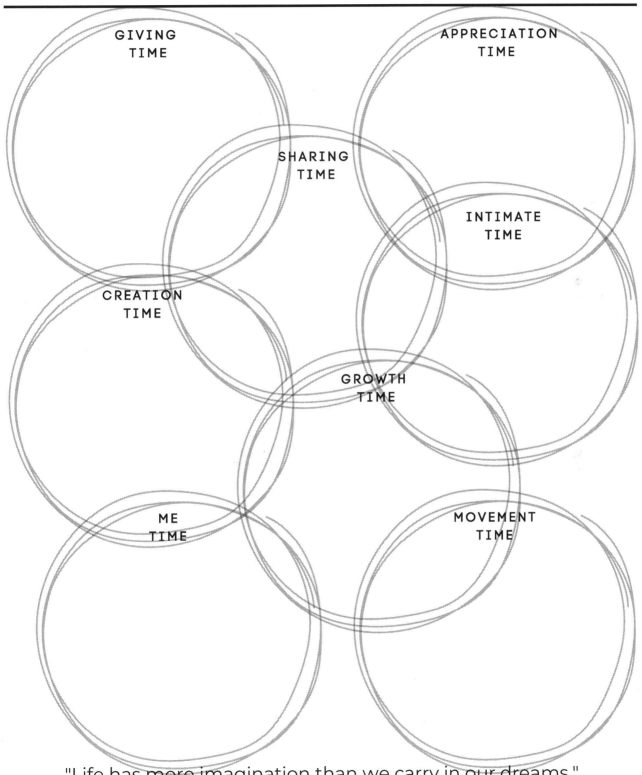

GIVING TIME

APPRECIATION TIME

SHARING TIME

INTIMATE TIME

CREATION TIME

GROWTH TIME

ME TIME

MOVEMENT TIME

"Life has more imagination than we carry in our dreams."
- Christopher Columbus ("Discoverer" of the "New" World)

MY 16 HOURS

TURNING YOUR 8 WORLDS INTO YOUR 8 TIME-ZONES

ACTIVITIES IN EACH ZONE - WHAT I WILL DO...

GIVING TIME

HELPING OTHERS - GIVING BACK - MEDITATE - PRAYER - REFLECT

SHARING TIME

FRIENDS - FAMILY - COLLEAGUES - STRANGERS

GROWTH TIME

MENTAL FOCUS - CONCENTRATION - LEARNING

INTIMATE TIME

TRUSTED PERSONAL CONNECTIONS

CREATION TIME

MAKING - BUILDING - DESIGNING - CREATING

ME TIME

ENJOYING THE THINGS THAT YOU LOVE - QUIET SOLITUDE

MOVEMENT TIME

MOVING YOUR BODY

APPRECIATION TIME

BEING THANKFUL & APPRECIATING YOUR PLACES OF MEANING

24 HOURS IS A DAY - TAKE AWAY 8 HOURS FOR SLEEP & YOU HAVE 16 HOURS
FOR YOU TO CHOOSE WHAT TO DO WITH. INCORPORATE TIME THAT REFLECTS
ALL YOUR WORLDS. NOT ENOUGH TIME?

DAILY ACTIVITIES

ACTIVITIES / ACTIONS	CROSSOVERS

( ) GIVING TIME

( ) GROWTH TIME

( ) SHARING TIME

( ) INTIMATE TIME

( ) CREATIVE TIME

( ) ME TIME

( ) MOVEMENT TIME

( ) APPRECIATION TIME

"Carpe diem" - Latin for "Seize the day!" or "Pluck the day for it is ripe."
Dating back to "Odes" by Horace in 23BC.
Humans have long seen the importance of "the Day".

MY 16 HOURS

TURNING YOUR WORLDS INTO YOUR TIME

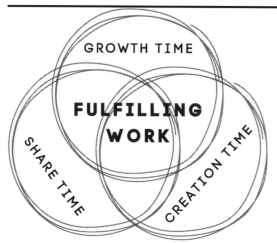

GROWTH TIME

FULFILLING WORK

SHARE TIME

CREATION TIME

WORK

COMBINE YOUR TIME ZONES - BY MAKING WORK FOCUSSED, SPENDING QUALITY TIME WITH COLLEAGUES AND LEARNING SOME NEW STUFF ON THE WAY - YOU ARE MAKING TIME FOR 3 OF YOUR WORLDS. SO INSTEAD OF WORK BEING WORK - MAKE IT WORK FOR YOU!

WHAT ARE YOUR WORLDS TO FULFILLING WORK?

EXERCISE

GO FOR A WALK / RUN / BIKE, THAT'S MOVEMENT & ME TIME. ADD IN A BUDDY; SHARING TIME; ADD IN GROWTH TIME IF YOU GO SOMEWHERE NEW OR PUSH YOURSELF. STOP FOR A MINUTE & APPRECIATE WHERE YOU ARE - FEEL YOUR BREATH, LOOK AROUND YOU WITH THANKS - THATS YOUR APPRECIATION TIME. WHAT'S YOUR COMBO?

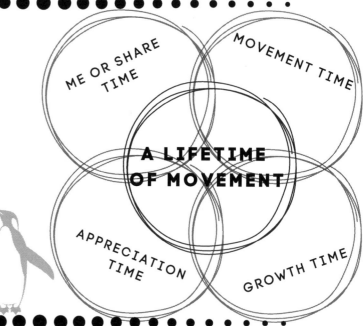

ME OR SHARE TIME

MOVEMENT TIME

A LIFETIME OF MOVEMENT

APPRECIATION TIME

GROWTH TIME

HOWEVER YOU STRUCTURE IT, MAKE CONSCIOUS TIME FOR ALL YOUR WORLDS. BY MAKING IT CONSCIOUS, YOU MAKE IT MINDFUL. LIFE WILL FEEL MORE PURPOSEFUL, FULFILLING & BALANCED -

MY TURN

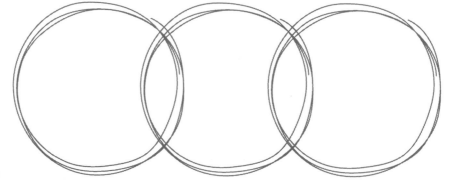

PENGUIN TIME?

EMPEROR PENGUINS - THE ONLY ANIMAL TO WITHSTAND THE COLD OF THE ANTARCTIC WINTER ABOVE GROUND (-60C / -76F + WINDCHILL) - COOPERATION, ADAPTATION & PURE TOUGHNESS!

MY 16 HOURS

CREATE & COMBINE YOUR WORLD TIME ZONES

"I don't much like boxes, I much prefer overlapping Venn diagrams"

CREATE (& SHARE) YOUR INGREDIENTS
FOR A HEALTHY RELATIONSHIP

SHARING TIME

GIVING TIME

HEALTHY RELATIONSHIPS START HERE

INTIMATE TIME

YOUR LIFE IS CIRCLUAR, IT GOES IN PATTERNS & RYTHMNS.
YOUR 16 HOURS HAPPENS DAY IN & OUT LIKE CLOCKWORK.
BY UNDERSTANDING YOUR PATTERNS, YOU UNDERSTAND YOUR LIFE.

"Life is a circle - the end of one journey is the beginning of the next."
- Joseph M. Marshall III (Teacher, Historian)

MY 16 HOURS

PRIORITIZE - IMPORTANCE & URGENCY

YOU WON'T TREAT ALL YOUR WORLD'S EQUALLY & YOU'LL PRIORITIZE & PREFER SOME OF YOUR WORLDS / TIMES OVER OTHERS. PRIORITIZE DOESN'T MEAN IGNORE. IT MEANS DECIDING WHAT'S MOST IMPORTANT / URGENT FOR YOUR PERSONAL NEEDS & TAKING ACTION.
PRIORITIZE - THEN MAKE TIME FOR ALL YOUR WORLDS.

WORLDS / TIMES / ACTIVITIES / ACTIONS

(ONE)

(TWO)

(THREE)

(FOUR)

(FIVE)

(SIX)

(SEVEN)

(EIGHT)

"As far as you can see; when you get there, you'll be able to see further." - Thomas Carlyle (British Writer, Philosopher, Teacher)

"The secret to living well and longer is;
eat half,
walk double,
laugh triple,
&
love without measure."

— Tibetan Proverb

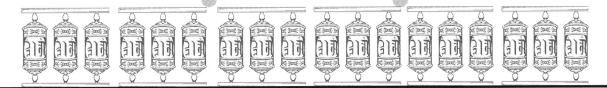

THE TIBETAN PRAYER WHEEL IS PART OF THE CULTURE OF THE
TIBETAN HIMALAYA. THE ROOF-TOP OF THE WORLD.
SPINNING THE WHEELS SENDS
MANTRAS / PRAYERS OUT INTO THE UNIVERSE.
YOU SPIN & RECITE THE MANTRA, CENTERING
YOURSELF, CONNECTING TO PLACE & GIVING
THANKS TO ALL THOSE THINGS SPINNING AROUND YOU.

ༀ་མ་ཎི་པ་དྨེ་ཧཱུྃ

USING THE DIAGRAM - ACCORDING TO YOUR PRIORITIES, ALLOCATE YOUR 16 HOURS TO YOUR 8 WORLD TIME-ZONES. THINK OF COMBINATIONS, ACTIVITIES & WAYS TO INCLUDE ALL YOUR WORLD TIME ZONES - GET CREATIVE & EXAMINE NEW OPPORTUNITIES.

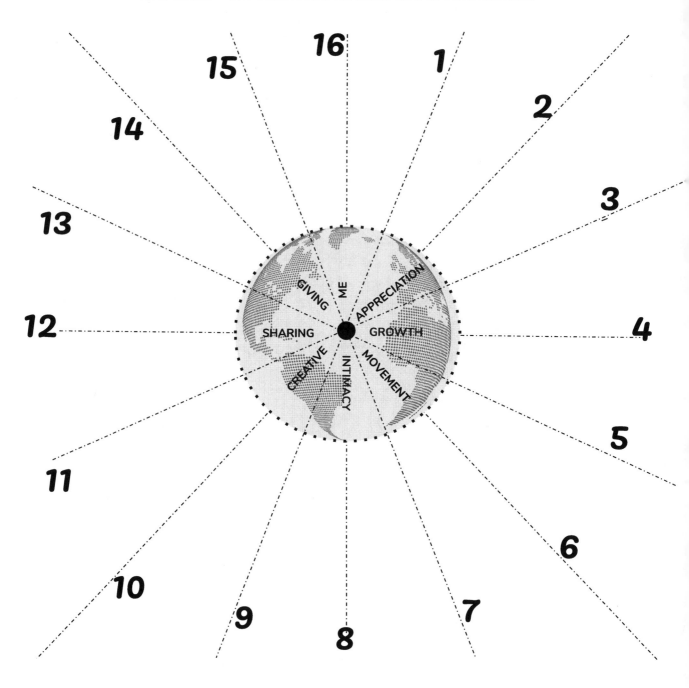

IT'S NOT ABOUT ACCOUNTING FOR EVERY SECOND OF THE DAY. IT'S SIMPLY A VISUAL GUIDE - A CONCEPTUALIZATION TO REMIND YOU TO LIVE INTENTIONALLY WITH GREATER PURPOSE & BALANCE

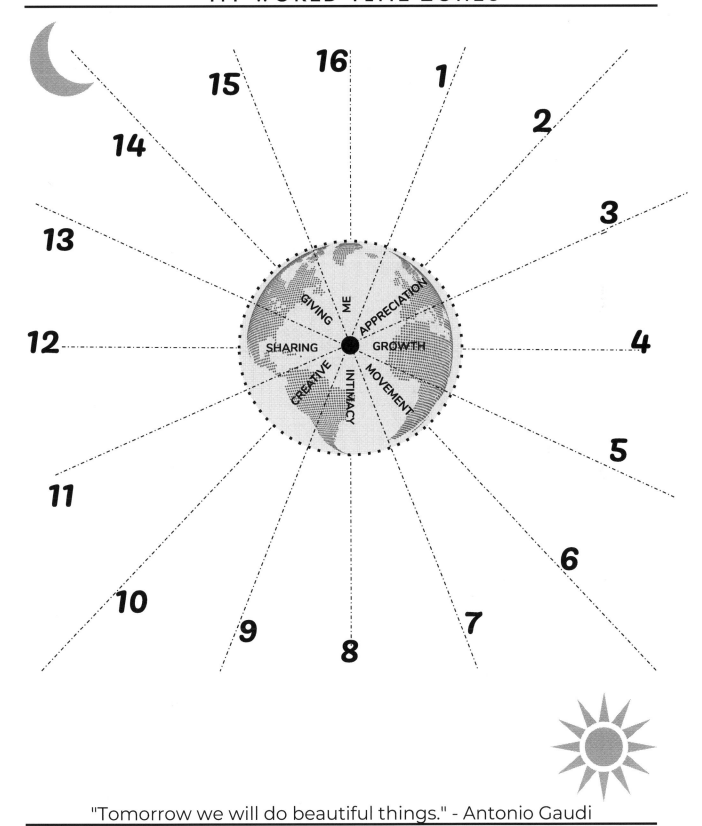

"Tomorrow we will do beautiful things." - Antonio Gaudi

MY 24 HOURS

8 HOURS
SLEEP
REST
RESTORE

16 HOURS
CREATE
ACT
GROW

4 + 8 + 4

HOURS   HOURS   HOURS

MORNING FOCUS   DAY FOCUS   EVENING FOCUS

+

FOCUS
WILLPOWER
CREATE
APPRECIATE
PLAN

DO
ACT
MEET
LEARN
PLAY

SHARE
GROW
REFRESH
REFLECT
CONNECT

−

'IDEAL' SCREENTIME - REDUCE EARLY MORNING / LATE EVENING

MY 4-8-4

MY 16 HOURS TO MY 4-8-4 FOCUS

MORNING FOCUS
5AM TO 9/10AM

FOCUS
WILLPOWER
CREATE
APPRECIATE
PLAN

4

IT'S A GOOD TIME FOR:

- FOCUS
- MEDITATION
- DEEP THOUGHT
- WORKING OUT
- CREATIVITY
- PLANNING

UNDERSTAND:
YOUR MORNING SETS UP YOUR DAY
USE YOUR 'GREATER' MORNING WILLPOWER
AVOID GOING STRAIGHT TO YOUR PHONE / EMAIL
MORNINGS ARE GOOD FOR MOVEMENT, MEDITATION, MINDFULNESS

DAY FOCUS
9AM TO 5PM

DO
ACT
MEET
LEARN
PLAY

8

- MEETINGS & PEOPLE
- ACTION
- TECHNOLOGY USAGE
- CREATING
- PRIORITIZING
- LEARNING
- MOVEMENT

REMEMBER:
TO TAKE BREAKS - SITTING OR STANDING TOO LONG
THE USES AND DISTRACTIONS OF TECH
MIDDAY MOVEMENT CAN HELP SUSTAIN ENERGY
CONCENTRATE YOUR SCREEN TIME HERE
MEET TO HELP RE-ENERGIZE
WHAT YOU EAT WILL HELP YOU GET THROUGH THE DAY

EVENING FOCUS
5PM TO 9/10PM

SHARE
GROW
REFRESH
REFLECT
CONNECT

4

- INTIMATCY
- SOCIALIZING
- PERSONAL (ME) TIME
- MEDITATION
- GROWTH / CREATIVITY
- RESEARCH
- REFLECTION

BEWARE OF:
LOWER WILLPOWER
FATIGUE / TIREDNESS
YOUR VICES
YOUR CAFFEINE INTAKE
YOUR BLUE LIGHT BEFORE BED (DEVICES)

THESE ARE GUIDELINES ONLY - TAILOR YOUR DAY BASED ON YOUR OPTIMAL WAKE / SLEEP TIME,
YOUR WORK & YOUR SCHEDULE - TO GET THE BEST OUT OF YOUR 16 HOURS, USE THE 4-8-4 METHOD.

MY 4-8-4

MY 16 HOURS TO MY 4-8-4 FOCUS

USING THE TEMPLATE, WHAT ARE THE TIMES BEST SUITED FOR YOU IN EACH OF THE FOCUS AREAS - BASED ON YOUR BODY CHEMISTRY & NEEDS - WHAT'S YOUR 4-8-4?

MORNING FOCUS
__AM TO __AM

4
FOCUS
WILLPOWER
CREATE
APPRECIATE
PLAN

THINGS / ACTIVITIES / IDEAS

DAY FOCUS
__AM TO __PM

8
DO
ACT
MEET
LEARN
PLAY

EVENING FOCUS
__PM TO __PM

4
SHARE
GROW
REFRESH
REFLECT
CONNECT

"Dost thou Love Life? Then do not squander time, for that is the stuff Life is made of." - Benjamin Franklin (US Founding Father)

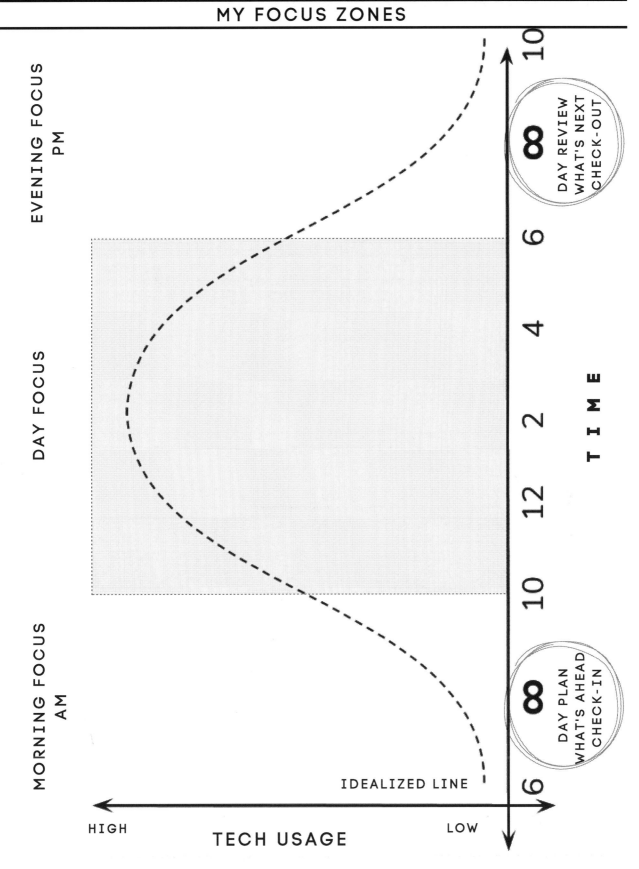

MY 16 HOURS

MY FOCUS ZONES

EVENING FOCUS
PM

DAY FOCUS

MORNING FOCUS
AM

8 DAY REVIEW
WHAT'S NEXT
CHECK-OUT

8 DAY PLAN
WHAT'S AHEAD
CHECK-IN

IDEALIZED LINE

TIME

6   10   12   2   4   6   8   10

HIGH

LOW

TECH USAGE

MY 4-8-4

	FOUR ☀	EIGHT	☾ FOUR
M			
T			
W			
T			
F			
S			
S			

"The two most powerful warriors are Patience and Time."
- Leo Tolstoy (Russian Literary Master - Author of "War & Peace")

MY 4-8-4

MY 16 HOURS TO MY 4-8-4 FOCUS

M

FOUR

EIGHT

FOUR

T

FOUR

EIGHT

FOUR

W

FOUR

EIGHT

FOUR

T

FOUR

EIGHT

FOUR

F

FOUR

EIGHT

FOUR

MY 16 HOURS : 4-8-4 FOCUS

EVENING
4

MORNING
4

16

15

14

13

12

11

10

9

8

1

2

3

4

5

6

7

GIVING

ME

APPRECIATION

SHARING

GROWTH

CREATIVE

INTIMACY

MOVEMENT

DAY
8

"I know of no single formula for success. But over the years I have observed that some attributes of leadership are universal and are often about finding ways of encouraging people to combine their efforts, their talents, their insights, their enthusiasm and their inspiration to work together."

— HRH Queen Elizabeth II

QUEEN ELIZABETH II IS THE HEAD OF STATE IN 16 COUNTRIES. AS THE WORLD'S LONGEST REIGNING MONARCH - ALMOST 70 YEARS; SHE HAS EARNED GLOBAL RESPECT THROUGH HER DETERMINED, SOLID & GRACEFUL LEADERSHIP OF THE BRITISH ROYAL FAMILY.

LEAD YOUR WORLDS WITH INTENTION... YOUR JOURNEY CONTINUES...

THE MANDALA

MANDALAS ARE FOUND THROUGHOUT MY PAGES.
'MANDALA' IS A SANSKRIT TERM MEANING 'CIRCLE'.
IN EASTERN RELIGIONS, MANDALAS ARE USED TO FOCUS ATTENTION & CREATE
A SACRED SPACE. THEY ALSO SYMBOLIZE THE UNIVERSE, THAT OF BALANCE,
WHOLENESS & INTERCONNECTION.

The circle is whole and complete.
Balance and harmony - it's really quite neat.
One unbroken line - it never ends.
Where it will it take you? Well that depends.

You check the compass to know your place.
You look at the clock to know your grace.
It's a journey - there and back.
Living in circles - what's your tack?

You surround yourself with a circle of friends.
You play games in circles and drive round bends.
The circle of life is kicked around.
Enjoy the ride & gather round.

On sunny days you look at her glow.
Round and round you will go.
On your journey around the sun.
One day comes and another one's done.

The seasons come and the seasons go.
The tides ebb and the tides flow.
The stars above spiraling around.
The planets are circles - gravity bound.

Where you'll land you'll never know.
On planet earth and the fruits you'll sow.
When you think it's finished and it's all done.
It continues on going... back where you begun.

GIVING TIME
INTIMATE TIME
MOVEMENT TIME
CREATIVE TIME
MY TIME
GROWTH TIME
SHARE TIME
APPRECIATION TIME

"The straight line belongs to men, the curved line to God."
- Antonio Gaudi (Catalan Architect - La Sagrada Familia)

MY CONTINUATION

Like any good book, there has to be an ending, well lucky for you, I'm not like any good book!
First of all, I'm a Great book (you saw the cover!), and secondly, this is only the beginning.
Remember the circle at the start, well now we come back to that again.
So this is not goodbye, it's a continuation.

As a little workbook with great ambitions, I have tried and will continue to try to help you look at life holistically. I'm a tool to use in your quest to continue your personal development at any time. Like a one-stop-shop or a guide you can keep coming back to. Use me at your own pace, in your own place of comfort.

I (this workbook) am not designed to replace in-person therapy or working with a coach or counselor. You can use me with these trusted professionals or in your own glorious solitude. You may also want to work with a trusted friend or even in a small group. It's amazing what you will learn from sharing your experiences and listening to the experiences of others.

As a book, I see life as a journey, as an adventure, a story, worlds to explore, things to try and opportunities to create. I also know you have the power in your hands to make a difference to your own life and I know you can create whatever it is you want to bring into being (within reason of course, humans are Great, but you have limitations).

The models, diagrams and concepts on my pages are helpful and insightful, but they are just what they are, concepts and models. Real life is messier, it doesn't adhere to straight lines, nor perfect circles. As I have shared these with you, I can't be sure how they will impact you, or help you. So I finish with this, with my list of the known. The things I can say for certain and without debate to be true. I hope what I have learned, can also be helpful to you, on your adventures ahead.

Here's what I know for certain:
- I am me and that's all I can be - I wouldn't trade my journey with anyone.
- I get 'butterflies' in my stomach and it's up to me to make them fly in formation.
- I feel all my emotions and I know they are temporary.
- I am talented, even though others don't always see it and I don't always feel it.
- I am creative and creation takes time.
- I am loved.
- There are others to support me (and sometimes I have to ask).
- I am not perfect (and that's a good thing).
- I make mistakes (thankfully, otherwise how would I learn and grow?)
- I know I will find solutions... eventually, they will come.
- That my values are important and they give me stability in knowing what they are.
- I remain hopeful... always!
- That hopelessness is the worst feeling I have experienced, ever!
- That being compassionate makes me stronger.
- I am forever grateful for what it has taken to get me here, to this point, right now!
- I want to live a Great Life - not an average life and that's my choice.
- The life I want does not come about without two ingredients; Intention and Effort!
- I am on my journey and what a spectacular adventure it is!

If you would like to keep in touch I can be found at www.greatape.ca
or follow us on Instagram @1greatape
Please give me a Review and share your experiences - To be continued...

MY **GREAT** LIFE8 INDEX

LIFE 8 INDEX - WHERE IT LIES

I MEAN NO OFFENCE TO ANYONE IN POINTING

THIS IS YOUR 'INDEX' FINGER IT COMES FROM LATIN "INDICO" 'TO POINT OUT' - IT'S YOUR POINTER.

IT CAN ALSO GET YOU INTO TROUBLE. KNOW WHAT IT MEANS WHEREVER YOU GO!

MY **GREAT** LIFE8 INDEX

LIFE8 INDEX - WHERE IT LIES... FURTHER

I WISH YOU PEACE & VICTORY ON YOUR JOURNEY!

THIS IS THE 'VICTORY SIGN' THE SIGN FOR PEACE NUMBER 2 & SEEN IN PHOTOS GLOBALLY!

JUST DON'T TURN IT AROUND OR THIS WILL ALSO GET YOU IN TROUBLE IN SOME PLACES!

ABOUT THE AUTHOR

I'm adding this page as you have a right to know where this information came from and who put it together. Two of my values are honesty and transparency, so this is me following them.

Hi there, my name is Mark, I was born and raised in Christchurch, New Zealand. When I grew up there in the 80s and 90s few people knew of her, now the world knows her name. Christchurch (Otautahi) gave me a great upbringing, located in the middle of one of the most beautiful islands on this planet, Te Waipounamu, the South Island of Aotearoa New Zealand.

I grew up exploring my native land, the wild and beautiful islands deep in the South Pacific. New Zealand is an inspirational country. Kiwis gave women the first vote, were first to climb the tallest mountain and may be the mightiest nation in world sport (I'm sure my Aussie mates would disagree). My kiwi roots are something of deep meaning to me and the values I have are largely thanks to the country I was born and raised; courageous, adventurous, respectful and humble :)

I have always been naturally very curious, my island home seemed far away from the rest of the world. As a kid, I would be out the door as soon as my mum would turn her back. So it was no surprise, after I graduated university, I was off on my own quest; To Explore Planet Earth.

So that's what I did, I followed my core value at the time, and for the next 20 years I would be on a global journey. It would take me across Asia and the Middle East, where I would live, teach and learn about its ancient traditions and religions. It would lead me to become a tour leader around Europe, North Africa, Russia and Turkey; educating groups while exploring their fascinating cultures, art and histories. From the Streets of Rome, to the Medinas of Marrakesh; my people-intensive roles, in many diverse places, led me to learn more about cultures and communication.

I love the natural world, I love to be outside and that's my own temple. It's where I find my inspiration and it's where my own adventures take me. I'm fascinated by the world's religions. I love history. I also appreciate an open mind and when people are genuine and respectful.
Respect is my first value and I would learn, is the fundamental value across all cultures.

My next move would be to North America, where my home base of Vancouver, Canada allowed me to work and travel across both Americas. From teaching in classrooms, to creating business deals across the Asia-Pacific. I explored the ancient civilizations from Peru to Mexico, as well as the modern capitals of States, Provinces and Territories across the continent.

I'm a teacher and also a student. I've always been fascinated with self-development, self improvement and creating a fulfilling life. I love food, nutrition, exercise and movement. Swim, bike and hike, I'll never stop exploring or learning, I will always ask "Why?"

I love teaching, passing on knowledge so others can discover their own wisdom. It's the reason I created this workbook. I have used worksheets with my diverse student and client population and they have really helped them find structure to their own thoughts, rather than the daunting blank page. I hope these help you find structure.

I'm not attached to any religion, nor specific philosophy, nor corporate or political interest; just Humanity. Curiosity, Creativity and Compassion. It's the 3 C's and a simple philosophy I choose to live by. No need to make it complex. The easier it is, the easier it is to follow. It's also why I created the company 'GREAT APE - Intentional Evolution', as we're all part of this wider family. Encouraging more effective communication across cultures and finding better ways to work together. Just to somehow make a positive difference.

My life, probably like your own, has been a rollercoaster ride. From the most epic of experiences, to the miseries of great loss. I hope the wisdom I have discovered, thus far, on my journey, can somehow be helpful to you, on yours.

The truth lies within.

Kia Kaha - Stay Strong and Hopeful!

LUA - MAKES ME SMILE EVERYDAY

MY DEDICATION

I DEDICATE THIS TO:

MY SISTER TAUGHT ME WHAT IT MEANS TO PUSH MY OWN BOUNDARIES & LIVE AUTHENTICALLY WITH PASSION & ADVENTURE.
THIS WOULDN'T HAVE BEEN POSSIBLE WITHOUT HER!

"Live your life with love and passion, and don't stop until you find them. Don't waste your time nor worry about trivial people or things. Find what you truly value and genuinely believe in and follow that path.. Believe me, that is your only option and nothing else will do."
- MY GREAT BIG SISTER, LEANNE (1977-2004)

Made in the USA
Columbia, SC
14 February 2021